'NORTH YORI

This guide book contains exact, but si
to combine visits to such well knov
Pickering, Helmsley, Rievaulx Abbey
dales, forests and high moorland country, that for the most part lies hidden beyond the more popular tourist routes.

The 'Main Circle' Route (Maps 1 – 14), shown on the Key Map opposite, covers 165 miles, and is far too long for a leisurely day's journey. We have therefore included 'link routes' to break this up into several smaller circles (see opposite). Each route, being circular, may of course be started at any point suitable to you.

HOW TO USE YOUR BOOK ON THE ROUTE

Each double page makes up a complete picture of the country ahead of you. On the left you will find a one inch to the mile strip map, with the route marked by a series of dashes. Direction is always from top to bottom, so that the map may be looked at in conjunction with the 'directions to the driver', with which it is cross referenced by a letter itemising each junction point. This enables the driver to have exact guidance every time an opportunity for changing direction occurs, even if it is only 'Keep straight, not left!'.

With mileage intervals shown, the driver should even have warning when to expect these 'moments of decision', and if a sign post exists we have used this to help you, with a 'Follow sign marked...' column. However re-signing is always in progress, and this may lead to slight differences in sign marking in some cases... So beware of freshly erected signs.

We have also included a description of the towns and villages through which you will pass, together with some photographs to illustrate the route.

To gain full enjoyment from your journeys, be prepared to leave your car as often as possible. We have tried to lead you away from the busy main roads whenever possible, but in certain places they prove to be unavoidable. We have referred briefly on page 39, to the subject of walking on the moors, and its attendant dangers, but be not dismayed, for there are boundless opportunities elsewhere for even the most inexperienced walker.

The North York Moors National Park contains some of the loneliest, and loveliest, countryside in England, and it makes a fine motoring area. However do not try to cover too many road miles in any one day, for there are so many opportunities for the quiet, relaxed visitor. So, drive slowly, stop often, and take time off to walk in sunlit dales, in great forests, and over the open moors... look at small churches, and magnificent abbeys, stop to chat in shops and inns, and above all... Don't Hurry!

COMPILED BY PETER, HELEN AND DAVID TITCHMARSH
PHOTOGRAPHY BY ALAN AND PETER TITCHMARSH

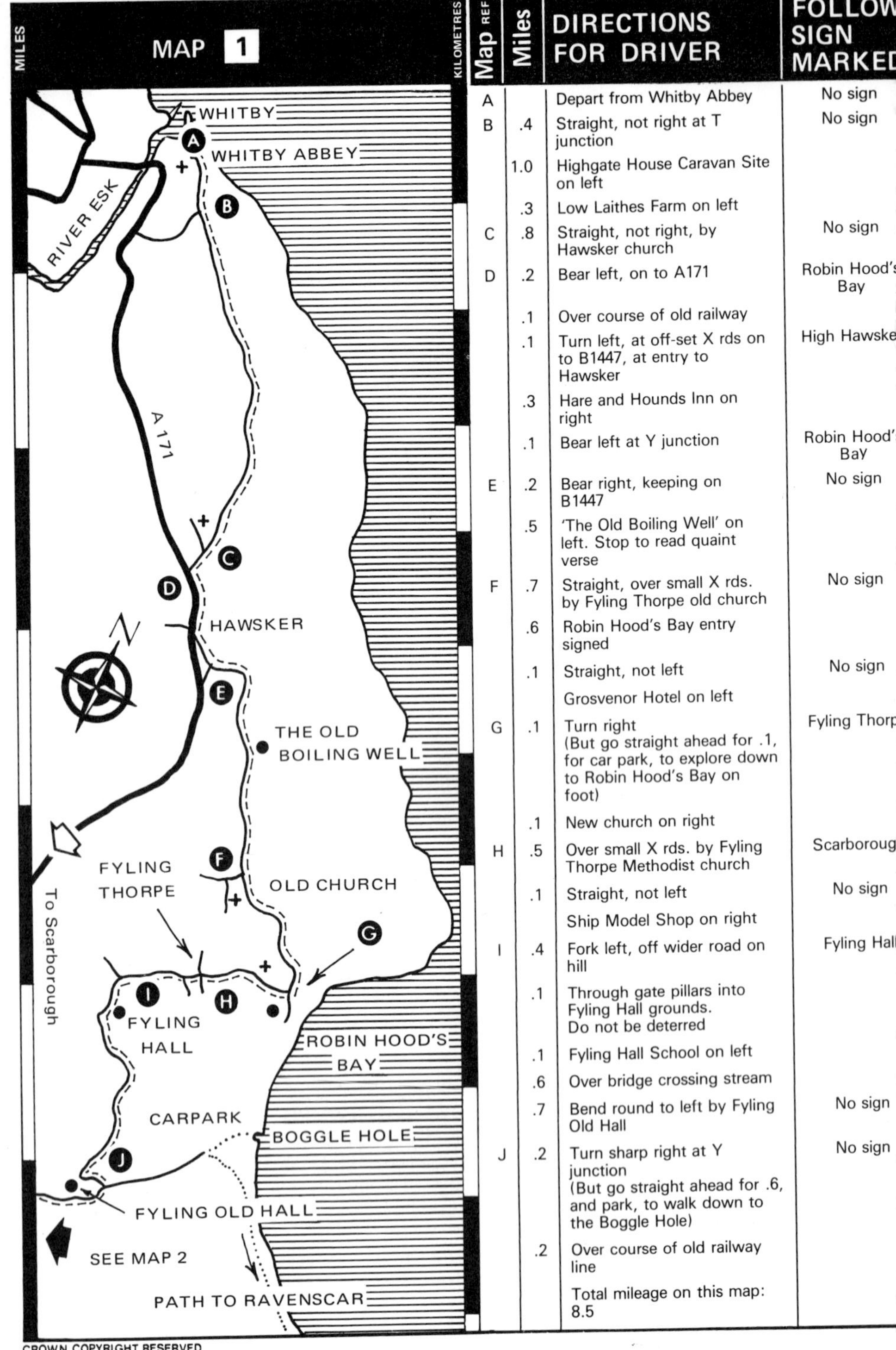

Map REF	Miles	DIRECTIONS FOR DRIVER	FOLLOW SIGN MARKED
A		Depart from Whitby Abbey	No sign
B	.4	Straight, not right at T junction	No sign
	1.0	Highgate House Caravan Site on left	
	.3	Low Laithes Farm on left	
C	.8	Straight, not right, by Hawsker church	No sign
D	.2	Bear left, on to A171	Robin Hood's Bay
	.1	Over course of old railway	
	.1	Turn left, at off-set X rds on to B1447, at entry to Hawsker	High Hawske
	.3	Hare and Hounds Inn on right	
	.1	Bear left at Y junction	Robin Hood's Bay
E	.2	Bear right, keeping on B1447	No sign
	.5	'The Old Boiling Well' on left. Stop to read quaint verse	
F	.7	Straight, over small X rds. by Fyling Thorpe old church	No sign
	.6	Robin Hood's Bay entry signed	
	.1	Straight, not left	No sign
		Grosvenor Hotel on left	
G	.1	Turn right (But go straight ahead for .1, for car park, to explore down to Robin Hood's Bay on foot)	Fyling Thorp
	.1	New church on right	
H	.5	Over small X rds. by Fyling Thorpe Methodist church	Scarboroug
	.1	Straight, not left	No sign
		Ship Model Shop on right	
I	.4	Fork left, off wider road on hill	Fyling Hal
	.1	Through gate pillars into Fyling Hall grounds. Do not be deterred	
	.1	Fyling Hall School on left	
	.6	Over bridge crossing stream	
	.7	Bend round to left by Fyling Old Hall	No sign
J	.2	Turn sharp right at Y junction (But go straight ahead for .6, and park, to walk down to the Boggle Hole)	No sign
	.2	Over course of old railway line	
		Total mileage on this map: 8.5	

LACES OF INTEREST ON THE ROUTE

Whitby

This is one of our favourite port towns, with a ong narrow harbour, overlooked on the east side by he great ruined abbey and the nearby parish church, nd on the west by Captain Cook's Monument, the Whalebone Arch, and a series of dignified Victorian seaside' hotels.

Whitby Abbey was founded in 657, but it was acked by the Danes just over two hundred years ater. Although it was re-established by the Benedictines in 1078, the existing remains only date from he 13th century. Despite the depredations of Henry 'III, a German bombardment in 1914, and the salt vinds of centuries, they present a most satisfying icture, with elemental ruins rising from smooth awns, and splendid views out over the harbour, and astwards along Sandsend Bay.

The parish church lies close below the Abbey, but o be truly appreciated, should be viewed from the reathless upper stages of Whitby's famous '199 teps', up from the harbour. It is a largely Norman uilding with a squat tower, and has a delightfully urnished Georgian interior, with box pews, a three ecker pulpit and little galleries everywhere.

On the other side of the harbour stands the handome monument to Captain Cook, who made his ome at Whitby between his historic voyages (his ouse in Grape Lane is marked by a plaque). Beside ie monument stands an arch made of two whale ones, a reminder of Whitby's great days as a base or whaling ships in the 18th and 19th centuries.

See also the steep little 18th and 19th century reets above the harbour, the lighthouse on the Vest Pier, and the interesting Art Gallery and Iuseum in Pannet Park, and, of course, spend as uch time as possible wandering along the busy uaysides.

lawsker

An unexceptional, windswept village with a mid-ictorian church, not of great interest to visitors.

he Old Boiling Well

An unusual little building roofed with two great one slabs. Stop to read the verse, which we can ıly describe as 'quaint North Country'.

ylingthorpe Old Church

Stands alone beside our road, looking out over the ne sweep of Robin Hood's Bay. Built in 1821, its terior is a wonderfully unspoilt example of late eorgian furnishing, with box pews, gallery and ree decker pulpit. Do not miss this.

obin Hood's Bay

Legend has it that Robin Hood once lived here in sguise, but this steep sloped little fishing village is r too attractive to require a folk hero to promote ; fame. Try to visit this 'Clovelly of the North' out season if you seek tranquillity. Don't overlook e 'new' church, which was designed by our vourite Victorian architect, G. E. Street, and ıich has some agreeable stained glass.

ıe Boggle Hole (see page 5)

1. *Whitby Habour*

2. *Cook Monument, Whitby*

3. *Whalebone Arch, Whitby*

4. *In Fylingthorpe Old Church*

5. *At Robin Hood's Bay*

6. *Fylingthorpe Old Church*

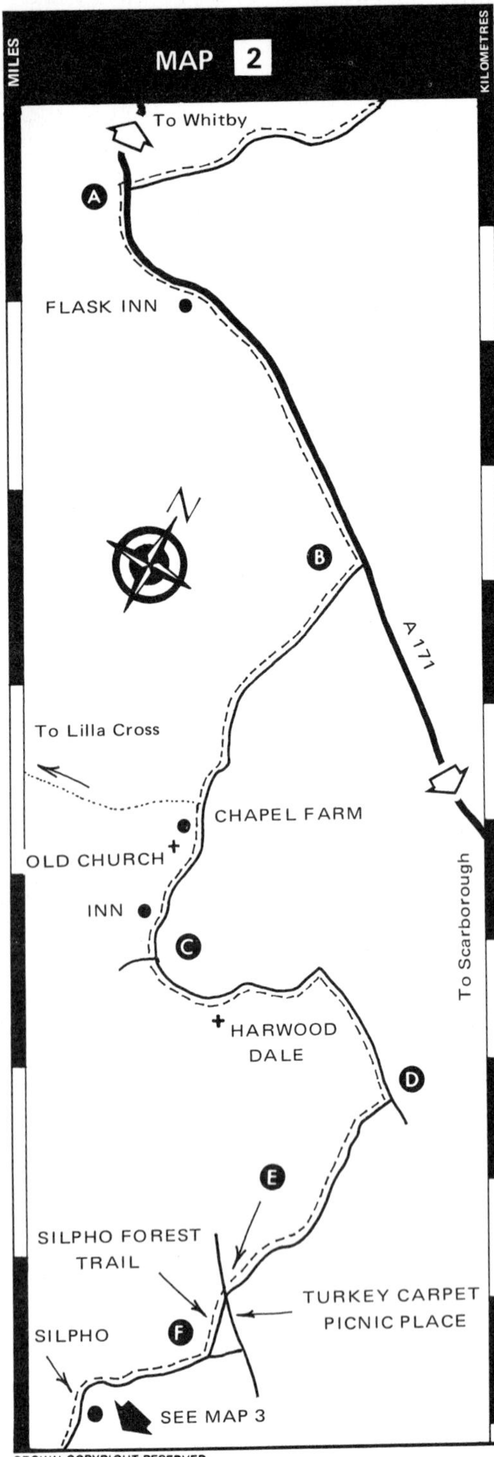

MILES

MAP 2

KILOMETRES

To Whitby

A

FLASK INN

B

A171

To Lilla Cross

CHAPEL FARM

OLD CHURCH

INN

C

To Scarborough

HARWOOD DALE

D

E

SILPHO FOREST TRAIL

TURKEY CARPET PICNIC PLACE

SILPHO

F

SEE MAP 3

Map REF	Miles	DIRECTIONS FOR DRIVER	FOLLOW SIGN MARKE
A	1.8	Turn left on to A171	Scarboroug
	.7	The Flask Inn and Petrol Station on right	
	1.1	Fine views ahead and to right	
B	.7	Turn right, off A171, and...	Harwood Da
		Enter Harwood Dale woodlands	
	1.9	Bridle way to Lilla on right. A fine moorland walk	
	.1	Chapel Farm on right. Coffee and Teas available at 'The Cruck House' adjoining the farm.	
		Ruins of Harwood Dale old chapel just visible from...	
	.1	Ruins of Harwood Dale old church just visible from road, in clump of trees to right immediately beyond Chapel Farm	
	.4	Path on right to Bybumblebee Hole, and...	
		Mill Inn on right	
C	.3	Bear left at T junction	Harwood D
	.3	Harwood Dale entry signed	
	.1	Church on right	
	.2	Methodist Chapel on left	
	.6	Moorland edge visible well over to right	
D	.8	Turn right at T junction	No sign
	.2	Past Thirley Cote Farm	
	.9	Track to Silpho Brow Farm on left	
		Woodlands now above us to right	
E	.3	Over offset X rds. by entry to Broxa Forest, and Turkey Carpet Picnic Place	No sign
	.2	Waymarked Forest Path on right (This is Silpho Forest Trail)	
F	.2	Bear right at T junction at end of woodlands	No sign
	.4	Silpho entry signed	
	.3	Bridle way to Low Dales on right	
		Total mileage on this map: 11.5	

PLACES OF INTEREST ON THE ROUTE

The Boggle Hole (see page 2)

Walk a few hundred yards from the car park (see Route Directions... Map 1, Point J), down a sheltered little valley. This soon opens out on to a wide beach (at low tide), with views of fine cliffs to the north. There is a bridle road southwards from the car park to Stoup Beck Sands, and a path onwards from there to Ravenscar (this forms part of the Cleveland Way... see page 39).

Harwood Dale

Here we enter the first of many Forestry Commission woodlands... Harwood Dale Forest, which is planted mainly with larch and pine. For details of the Forestry Commission's work in the whole area, we recommend the excellent Forestry Commission guide entitled 'North Yorkshire Forests' also the very useful 'Pickering District Forest Map'. Both are obtainable from the Forestry Commission at 42, Eastgate, Pickering.

Bridle Road to Lilla Cross

Lilla Cross lies about five miles from our road at Chapel Farm (see Route Directions), and an exploration of it makes a fine moorland walk. Lilla was killed while preventing the attempted assassination of King Edwin in 626, and the cross marks his burial place. Ensure that you have the Ordnance Survey One Inch Tourist Map of the North York Moors... an ideal complement to this guide at all times, but especially necessary when walking away from the road in moorland areas.

Chapel Farm

Coffee, teas and farm produce are available at the adjoining Cruck House. The owners will also allow visitors to walk over to the ruins of Harwood Dale Old Chapel, a little 17th century building just beyond the farm. This is a roofless shell, but there are handsome 18th century gravestones in its churchyard.

Harwood Dale Church

A rather uninteresting little Victorian building, but there are pleasant views from the churchyard across the valley to Broxa Forest. There is also an attractive little shelter built into the churchyard wall, in memory of those who did not return from the 14 – 18 War... What a grim number for such a quiet place to have provided for the slaughter.

Turkey Carpet Picnic Place—Broxa Forest

A pleasant picnic area beside our road, thoughtfully provided by the Forestry Commission... but, why Turkey Carpet? Apparently this may have been derived from the Danish name Thurkil, as the old road Thurkilsti comes down the scarp slope at Turkey Nab.

Silpho Forest Trail

The 'Long Trail' of three miles may be shortened to one and three quarters, but for details you should obtain the descriptive leaflet from the Forest Commission, 42, Eastgate, Pickering.

Silpho

Small scattered village, with a pleasant bridle way down to Lowdales (see page 7). No church, no inn.

1. In Harwood Dale Forest

2. Ruined Chapel, Harwood Dale

3. Broxa Forest, from Harwood Dale Churchyard

4. Turkey Carpet Picnic Place

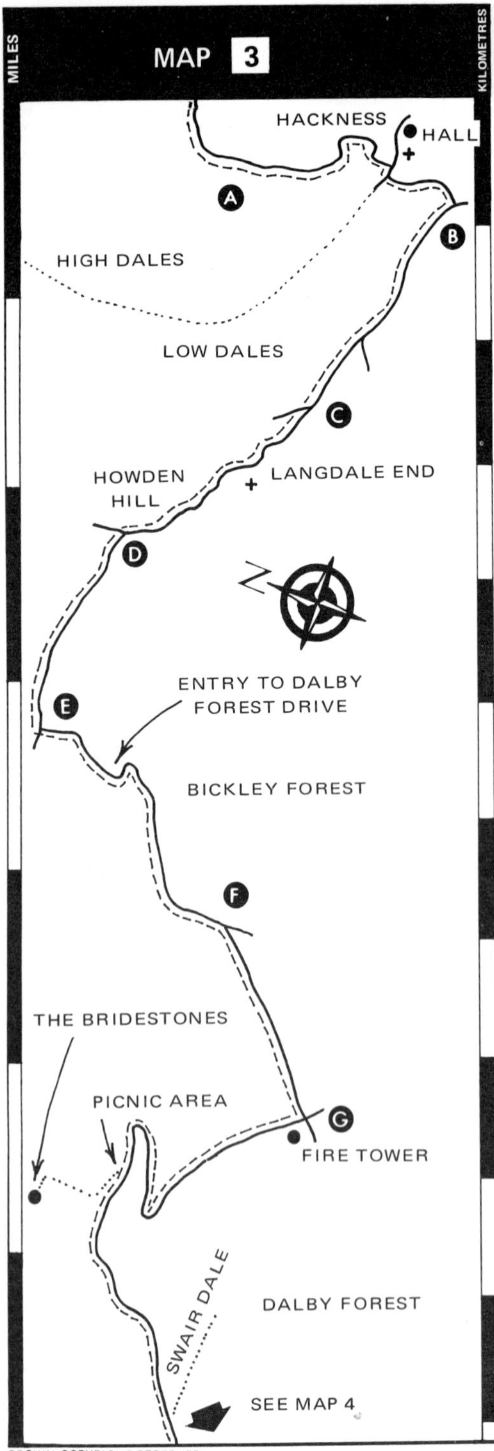

MILES

MAP 3

KILOMETRES

HACKNESS
HALL
HIGH DALES
LOW DALES
HOWDEN HILL
LANGDALE END
ENTRY TO DALBY FOREST DRIVE
BICKLEY FOREST
THE BRIDESTONES
PICNIC AREA
FIRE TOWER
SWAIR DALE
DALBY FOREST
SEE MAP 4

Map REF	Miles	DIRECTIONS FOR DRIVER	FOLLOW SIGN MARKE
	.7	Pleasant open road with views down to Hackness	
	.2	Down steep hill with hairpin bends, into pleasant woodlands	
	.2	Hackness entry signed	
A	.1	Turn right at T junction (But turn left if you wish to visit church, and explore up wooded valley beyond)	Forge Valle
	.1	Over bridge, and... Bear sharp left (Walk straight ahead if you wish to explore up High and Low Dales)	No sign
	.1	Lake alongside on left	
B	.2	Bear right by Red House Field Study Centre	Troutsdale
	.2	Hackness Grange Hotel on left	
	.5	River Derwent below us on left	
	.3	Straight, not left at Y junction	Broxa
C	.4	Straight, not right at Y junction	Langdale Er
	.4	Over bridge crossing River Derwent, and... Langdale End Post Office on left	
	.1	Church on left	
	.2	The Moorcock Inn on left	
	.1	Howden Hill above right	
D	.2	Straight, not right	No sign
	.2	'The Manor House' on left	
	.1	Attractive ford down left	
	.4	Bickley Forest entry signed	
	.5	Pleasant open road with fine forest view to right	
E	.4	Turn left at T junction and... Dalby Forest entry signed	'Forest Driv Low Dalby
	.5	Past Forest Park Sign	
	.5	Toll Charge Point, with Ticket Meter	
	.9	Bear right at Y junction	No sign
F	1.0	Turn right by fire tower	No sign
G	1.6	Over Staindale Beck at entry to Staindale	
	.4	Good parking and Picnic Area, with... Path on right to the Bridestones	
	1.6	Small track down right to the Staindale Beck Track up Swair Dale to left (not signed)	
		NOT SHOWN ON MAP	
	1.1	Snever Dale Forest Trail Car Park on left	
	.2	Snever Dale Car Park up left... Toilets, and woodland walks. Picnicking possible at streamside over to right Total mileage on this map: 13.4	

PLACES OF INTEREST ON THE ROUTE

Hackness

Delightful estate village in a deep wooded valley, with a handsome 18th century mansion... Hackness Hall... in a modest park, with small lake, and a most interesting church with Anglo-Saxon origins. This has an Anglo-Saxon chancel arch, but of even greater interest are the two pieces of an Anglo-Saxon cross... the only remaining evidence in stone, of a nunnery which existed here in the 8th century, before its destruction by the Danes in 869. See also the choir stalls with their carved misericords, the medieval font cover, and several interesting wall monuments... especially the monument to Mrs. Johnstone by Sir Francis Chantrey, the sculptor who produced so many extraordinarily poignant memorials.

Low Dales and High Dales

Park just beyond Hackness if you wish to explore on foot up either of these dales. The road, while being a delight for walkers, is certainly not suitable for the motorist. It is possible to walk up Low Dales to Silpho or Broxa Forest (see page 5).

Langdale End

This minute village beneath conical Howden Hill marks our entry into the extensive Langdale Forest, all of which lies to the right of our road. It has an uninteresting little Victorian church, and The Moorcock, an inn of great character, which time has passed completely by... long may it remain so.

Dalby Forest Drive

This is a 'forest road' which has been upgraded for public use, as a toll road, and we hope that no White Horse reader will begrudge the Forestry Commission the modest charge involved. May we suggest that, if budgets are tight, the next round of ice creams (or beers) is cheerfully sacrificed.

As the notice at the entry proclaims the drive is made up of ten miles of forest scenery, forest walks and trails, picnic places, and forest wildlife. Dalby Forest is part of the largest man-made forest area in England, apart from Kielder Forest, and provides many fine walking opportunities. The drive itself is inevitably busy at peak holiday times.

The Bridestones

There is a pleasant parking and picnic area in the valley below the Bridestones. The stones themselves are a fascinating series of tor-like outcrops poised on the top of steep slopes, looking out westwards across a valley. To reach them follow a waymarked trail, which starts over to the right of our road, at the far end of the Picnic Area. There is a well carved map-sign giving route directions, at a stile where the trails begin. Do not miss the attractive walk up through steep woodland and out over the open moor. (A Nature Trail leaflet is available from Information Centres or the National Trust, York.)

Snever Dale Forest Trail (see page 23)

1. Hackness Church

2. Bridestones Sign

3. Picnic Area below The Bridestones

4. The Low Bridestones

5. Forest Museum, Low Dalby (see pp. 8-9)

MILES

MAP 4

KILOMETRES

LOW DALBY
FOREST MUSEUM, ETC.
DALBY FOREST DRIVE ENDS
To Scarborough
ELLERBURN
To Whitby
THORNTON DALE
A 169
NORTH YORK MOORS RAILWAY
A 170
CASTLE
MUSEUM
A 169
To Flamingo Park
PICKERING
MIDDLETON
AISLABY
WRELTON
N
SEE MAP 5

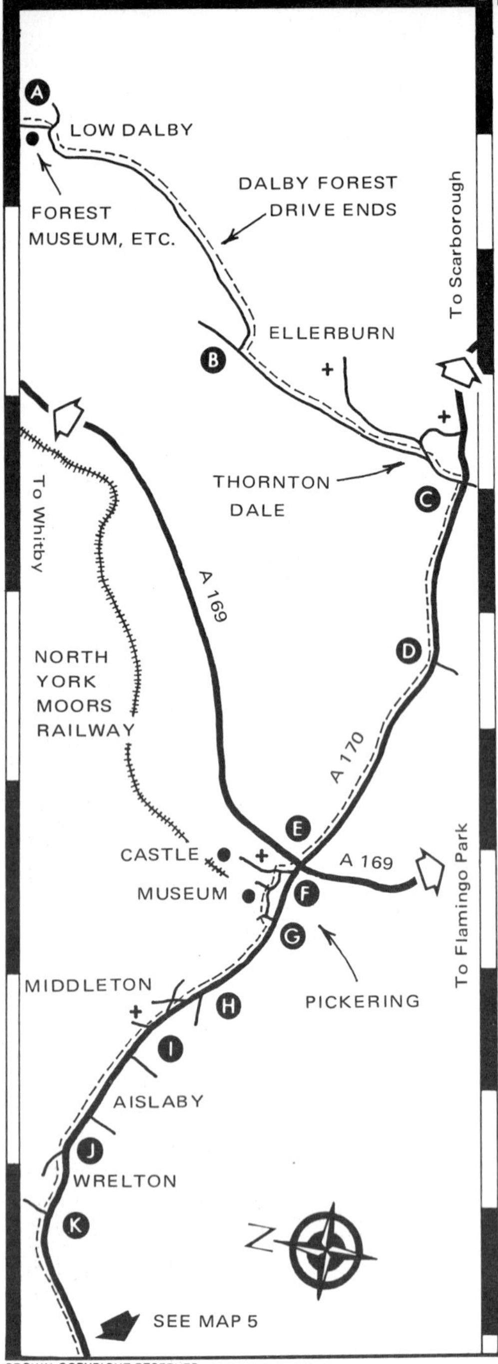

Map REF	Miles	DIRECTIONS FOR DRIVER	FOLLOW SIGN MARKEI
	.3	Car Park on right, and... Forestry Commission Information Centre, Forest Museum and Wildlife Display on right, and...	
A		Turn right at T junction by Low Dalby Post Office	No sign
	.1	Cross Dalby Beck	
	.5	Pleasant open hillside, with fine views across valley	
	.8	Forest Drive ends	
B	.7	Turn left at T junction	Thornton Dal
	1.1	Steep hill signed	
	.1	Down hill through woods	
	.2	Straight, not left at Thornton Dale entry sign (But turn left and fork left if you wish to visit Ellerburn... .8)	No sign
C	.2	Turn right in Thornton Dale, on to A170 (But turn left if you wish to visit church)	Thirsk
D	.9	Straight, not left, keeping on A170	No sign
	.8	Pickering entry signed	
E	.6	Over roundabout and...	Thirsk
		Turn right, almost immediately, by Hopkinson's Shop and immediately	Pickering Cast
		Fork left by green, and...	No sign
F		Straight, not right (But turn right if you wish to visit Castle)	Beck Isle Museum
	.1	Straight, not right, by Midland Bank	Thirsk
	.1	Over bridge, and...	
		Beck Isle Museum on right	
		Bear left by small triangular green, and...	No sign
G	.1	Turn right, re-joining A170 (Follow out of Pickering on A170, and keep on A170 for 4 miles)	No sign
H	.7	Bear right, keeping on A170	Thirsk
	.2	Straight, not right, at entry to Middleton	No sign
I	.4	Straight, not right by the New Tavern Inn	No sign
	.3	Aislaby entry signed	
	.1	Blacksmith's Arms	
		Restaurant and a gift shop on right	
J	.4	Bear left at Y junction, keeping on A170	Thirsk
	.3	Wrelton entry signed	
K	.1	Straight, not right by the Buck Inn	No sign
		Total mileage on this map: 9.1	

PLACES OF INTEREST ON THE ROUTE

Forestry Commission Information Centre and Museum — Low Dalby (See photo p. 7.)
Do not pass through Low Dalby without visiting this. There is a modest, but most effective display, and this will certainly help you to appreciate the complexity of the modern forester's tasks, and the extent of the wildlife that, with care and patience, may be spotted in the North Yorkshire Forests.

Ellerburn
This is an agreeably quiet little village, in a valley with beech woods, with a tea garden beside a small stream... all rather reminiscent of the Chilterns thirty or forty years ago. The church has virtually no tower, but its interior, having escaped the attentions of the more ruthless restorers, is still full of atmosphere. See especially the handsome 18th century pulpit, the old stone floors, and the two interesting cross heads, at least one of which reveals Danish influence (10th century).

Thornton Dale
Beautiful village astride the busy A170, with many small bridges over the little Thornton Beck, which is itself overlooked by elegant houses and thatched cottages, and further enlivened by ever moving ducks. There is an 'Old Grammar School' and almshouses, and a village green complete with market cross and stocks. The interior of the largely 14th century church has been rather heavily restored, but it contains two interesting monuments.

Pickering
A busy market centre which has not allowed its genuine flavour to be overshadowed by tourism. Explore its narrow, sloping streets away from the main road... Visit the church to look at the splendid medieval wall paintings (subjects include the Martyrdom of St. Catherine; St. Christopher; St. George and the Dragon; and John the Baptist's head on a charger... all the old Medieval favourites... Look at the ruined castle, (dating from the 12th century) on the north of the town, with fine views out over well mown lawns from its central motte... Visit the Beck Isle Museum, an attractive little 18th century building, housing an interesting folk collection. The North York Moors Railway has its southern terminus at Pickering... for details see page 35. There is a National Park Information Centre at the Station.

Middleton
An unexceptional village, with a dignified Georgian 'Hall', and a church standing well back from the road. The tower is undoubtedly Saxon, and inside there is a pleasing 18th century pulpit, one choir stall with a misericord, and the fragments of no fewer than three Angle-Danish crosses.

Aislaby
Busy with traffic, but has a pleasant restaurant, The Blacksmith's Arms, and a gift shop close by.

1. At Thornton Dale

2. Pickering Castle

3. Beck Isle Museum, Pickering

4. Daffodil Time at Pickering

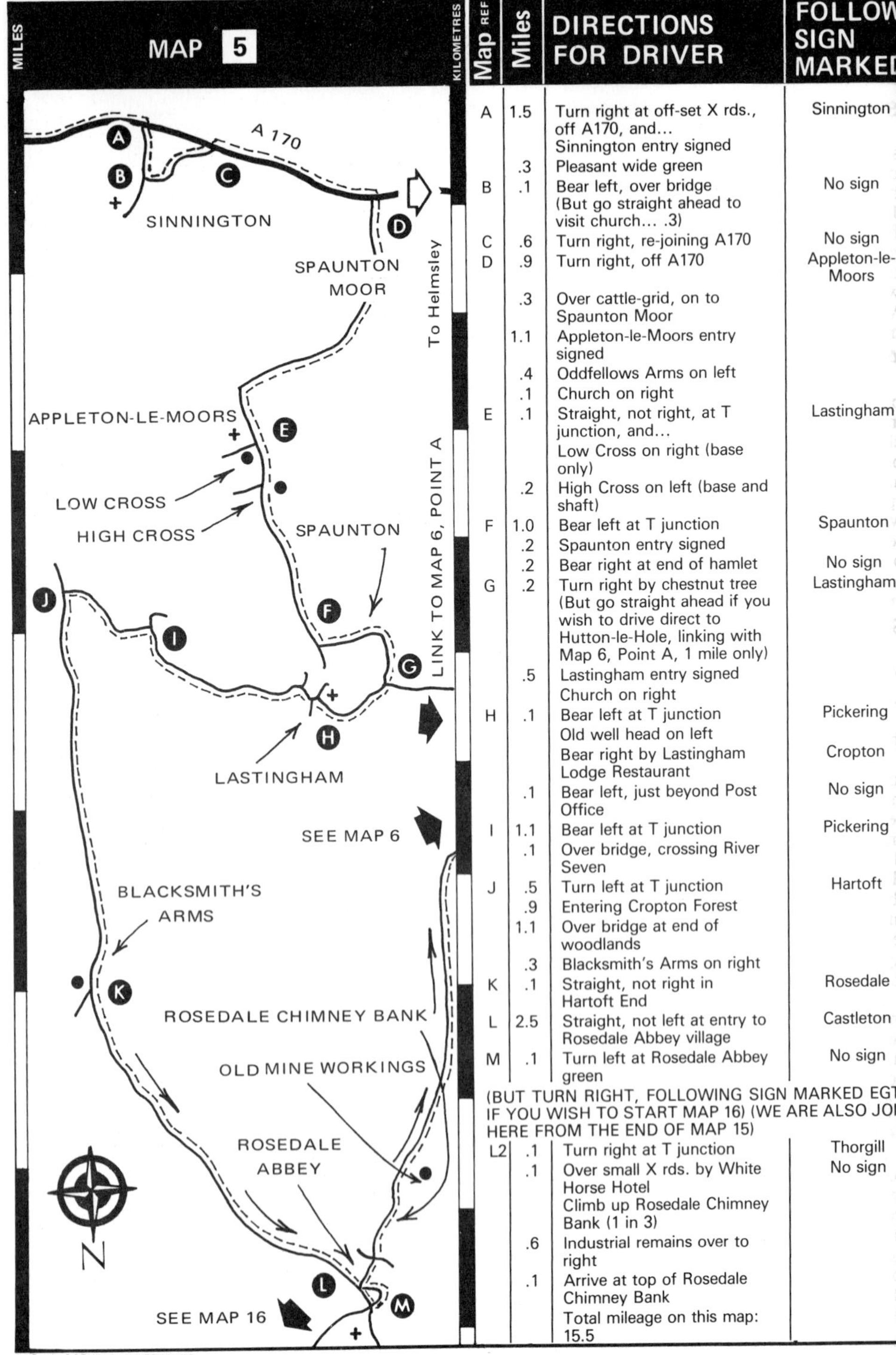

Map REF	Miles	DIRECTIONS FOR DRIVER	FOLLOW SIGN MARKED
A	1.5	Turn right at off-set X rds., off A170, and... Sinnington entry signed	Sinnington
	.3	Pleasant wide green	
B	.1	Bear left, over bridge (But go straight ahead to visit church... .3)	No sign
C	.6	Turn right, re-joining A170	No sign
D	.9	Turn right, off A170	Appleton-le-Moors
	.3	Over cattle-grid, on to Spaunton Moor	
	1.1	Appleton-le-Moors entry signed	
	.4	Oddfellows Arms on left	
	.1	Church on right	
E	.1	Straight, not right, at T junction, and... Low Cross on right (base only)	Lastingham
	.2	High Cross on left (base and shaft)	
F	1.0	Bear left at T junction	Spaunton
	.2	Spaunton entry signed	
	.2	Bear right at end of hamlet	No sign
G	.2	Turn right by chestnut tree (But go straight ahead if you wish to drive direct to Hutton-le-Hole, linking with Map 6, Point A, 1 mile only)	Lastingham
	.5	Lastingham entry signed Church on right	
H	.1	Bear left at T junction Old well head on left	Pickering
		Bear right by Lastingham Lodge Restaurant	Cropton
	.1	Bear left, just beyond Post Office	No sign
I	1.1	Bear left at T junction	Pickering
	.1	Over bridge, crossing River Seven	
J	.5	Turn left at T junction	Hartoft
	.9	Entering Cropton Forest	
	1.1	Over bridge at end of woodlands	
	.3	Blacksmith's Arms on right	
K	.1	Straight, not right in Hartoft End	Rosedale
L	2.5	Straight, not left at entry to Rosedale Abbey village	Castleton
M	.1	Turn left at Rosedale Abbey green	No sign

(BUT TURN RIGHT, FOLLOWING SIGN MARKED EGT IF YOU WISH TO START MAP 16) (WE ARE ALSO JOI HERE FROM THE END OF MAP 15)

Map REF	Miles	DIRECTIONS FOR DRIVER	FOLLOW SIGN MARKED
L2	.1	Turn right at T junction	Thorgill
	.1	Over small X rds. by White Horse Hotel Climb up Rosedale Chimney Bank (1 in 3)	No sign
	.6	Industrial remains over to right	
	.1	Arrive at top of Rosedale Chimney Bank	
		Total mileage on this map: 15.5	

ᴾLACES OF INTEREST ON THE ROUTE

Sinnington

We were lucky enough to visit Sinnington in spring time, and were delighted with daffodils beneath the trees on the wide greens, and on the banks of the River Seven, above its broad arched 18th century bridge. In contrast, the little medieval foot bridge, now high and dry on the green, looked rather sad; but we liked the little, restored church on the slopes of the hill beyond, beside a barn which was once the great hall of a medieval manor house. More Anglo-Saxon and Anglo-Danish cross fragments in the church.

Appleton-le-Moors

Has one long, wide street overlooked by several pleasant 18th and early 19th century houses, and an inn called the Oddfellows Arms. The Victorian church does not look very appetizing from the outside, but do not be deterred. J. L. Pearson, the architect of Truro Cathedral, has created here a splendidly elaborate interior, with colourful rose window, and beautifully painted figures on pulpit, reredos and chancel apse... all in delicate reds and pinks.

There are the remains of two medieval wayside crosses beyond the village.

Spaunton

Pleasant hamlet on the very edge of the moors, with wide grass verges and a house dated 1695.

Lastingham

Exceptionally pretty village tucked away beneath the moors. Bishop Cedd is believed to have founded a monastery here in 654, and died here of the plague some ten years later. As with so many other monastic houses in the north and east, this was destroyed by the Danes in the 9th century, and the unique and beautiful crypt beneath Lastingham church dates from a re-building of 1078, as a resting place for St. Cedd's bones. Much of the church above the crypt also dates from the Norman period, and the rest is due to an unusually sensitive restoration by our friend, J. L. Pearson (see Appleton... above). Do not miss this wholly pleasing church.

See also St. Cedd's Well (well head not of great antiquity), the Blacksmith's Arms, the Lastingham Lodge Restaurant, with its delightful verse carved on the door lintel, and the bright little Post Office stores... all very worthwhile.

Rosedale Abbey (see page 31)

Rosedale Chimney Bank

This is a VERY steep (1 in 3) climb out of the Rosedale Abbey, and drivers are advised to keep in lowest gear. Within a short distance of the top there are extensive 'industrial remains' over to our right. This was where ironstone was loaded on to trains of the old Rosedale Railway, which ran from here north westwards, right over the moor to Battersby, where it linked with the main line. It finally closed in 1929, after running for eighty years.

1. Spring Time at Sinnington

2. The Crypt, Lastingham

3. Cedd's Well, Lastingham

4. Our Road Up Rosedale

5. Ironstone Loading Point, Rosedale Chimney

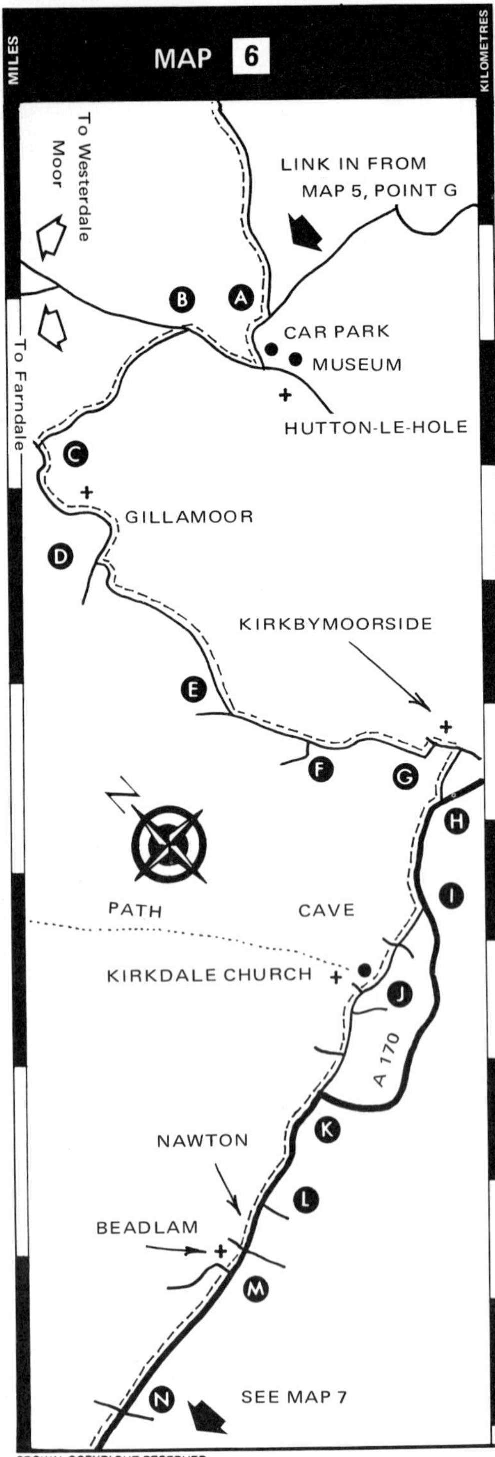

MILES

MAP 6

KILOMETRES

To Westerdale Moor

LINK IN FROM MAP 5, POINT G

To Farndale

A B

CAR PARK

MUSEUM

HUTTON-LE-HOLE

C

GILLAMOOR

D

KIRKBYMOORSIDE

E F G H

PATH

CAVE

I

KIRKDALE CHURCH

J

A 170

K

NAWTON

L

BEADLAM

M

N

SEE MAP 7

Map REF	Miles	DIRECTIONS FOR DRIVER	FOLLOW SIGN MARKE
	2.4	Over small bridge	
A	.6	Bear right on to wider road at Y junction	No sign
	.1	Hutton-le-Hole entry signed	
		Car Park on left. (Please use this, and explore Hutton-le-Hole on foot)	
	.2	Turn right	Farndale
B	.5	Fork left (But fork right if you wish to explore up Farndale, or up over Farndale and Westerdale Moors, linking on to Map 12 at Westerdale)	Gillamoor
	1.0	Over bridge	
	.1	Car park on right	
C	.1	Straight, not right	Gillamoor
	.6	Gillamoor entry signed	
		Church on left	
D	.2	Turn left by Royal Oak Inn	Kirkbymoorsi
E	1.2	Bear left at Y junction	Kirkbymoorsi
F	.5	Straight, not right	No sign
	.4	Kirkbymoorside entry signed	
G	.5	Bear right into the High Market Place	No sign
		King's Head on right	
	.1	Turn right in the square by the White Horse	Helmsley
H	.4	Turn right, on to A170	No sign
I	.4	Turn right, off A170 (WATCH FOR THIS WITH CARE)	'St. Gregory Minster'
	.2	Over X rds.	Kirkdale
	.3	(Cave on right just before ford)	
		Through ford	
J	.1	Straight, not right (But turn down right if you wish to visit Kirkdale church... .1 only)	No sign
	.1	Straight, not left	No sign
	.2	Straight, not right	No sign
K	.4	Bear right, re-joining A170 (Keep on A170 for 5 miles)	No sign
	.3	Nawton entry signed	
L	.3	Straight, not left	No sign
	.1	Rose and Crown on left	
	.1	Over X rds.	Helmsley
		Beadlam entry signed	
		Church on right	
M	.1	Straight, not right	No sign
	.3	Good parking on left	
	.3	Good parking on right	
N	.6	Over X rds.	Thirsk
		Total mileage on this map: 12.7	

PLACES OF INTEREST ON THE ROUTE

Hutton-le-Hole

This is scattered prettily around a wide irregular green, itself divided by the little Hutton Beck; and were it not for the red tiled roofs, the stone cottages and sheep clipped turf could almost be in Cotswold country. The village lies beneath high Spaunton Moor, close to the entry to Farndale, and is much visited at all holiday times. Do not miss the interesting Ryedale Folk Museum, situated in old farm buildings, and housing a collection of rural byegones, including an Elizabethan glass furnace, a blacksmith's shop and a wagon park. PLEASE USE CAR PARK AND WALK INTO VILLAGE.

Farndale

If you come this way in spring, and can manage to avoid the almost unavoidable crowds, fork right at Point B, to explore up Farndale. This will enable you to follow the specially signed 'Daffodil Route', to Low Mill (3.7 miles), from where you can walk to see the wild daffodils. It is a pity that it has all had to be so organised, but there appears to be no alternative where these tourist 'honey-pots' are concerned. Please do NOT pick daffodils.

Gillamoor

Has a wide street with no special features, apart from the modest Royal Oak Inn. The little church was built in 1802, but its pleasant interior contains several 17th century features.

Kirkbymoorside

An old market town, now much overshadowed by Pickering; with wide streets, quiet squares, and a bewildering number of inns (see especially the half timbered porch of the Black Swan, dated 1634). There is a pleasant church, with a 15th century two storeyed porch and a handsome east end by Sir Giles Gilbert Scott.

Kirkdale

Beautifully quiet valley with small stream flowing through woodlands and a path leading northwards up the dale for at least three miles. In Kirkdale Cave (see Route Directions) in 1821, were discovered the bones of hyenas, lions, rhinoceros and mammoth, but it is very hard to visualize this tranquil valley once alive with tropical wildlife.

However most visitors to Kirkdale come to see its beautiful little church, lying a short distance up the valley. This is basically an Anglo-Saxon building, although the tower was added in 1827 and the chancel re-built in 1881. See especially the tall Anglo-Saxon west doorway, and the very well known Anglo-Saxon sun-dial, with its inscription clearly indicating that the church was re-built in the time of Edward (the Confessor) and Tosti (Tostig) the Earl... about 1060. DON'T MISS THIS DELIGHTFUL BUILDING.

Nawton and Beadlam

These two villages lie on the A170, and join each other at the cross roads by Beadlam church. The road is just too busy to justify a halt here. Let's move on to Helmsley...

1. Hutton-le-Hole

2. Kirkbymoorside Church

3. The Black Swan, Kirkbymoorside

4. Kirkdale Church

5. Saxon Sundial, Kirkdale Church

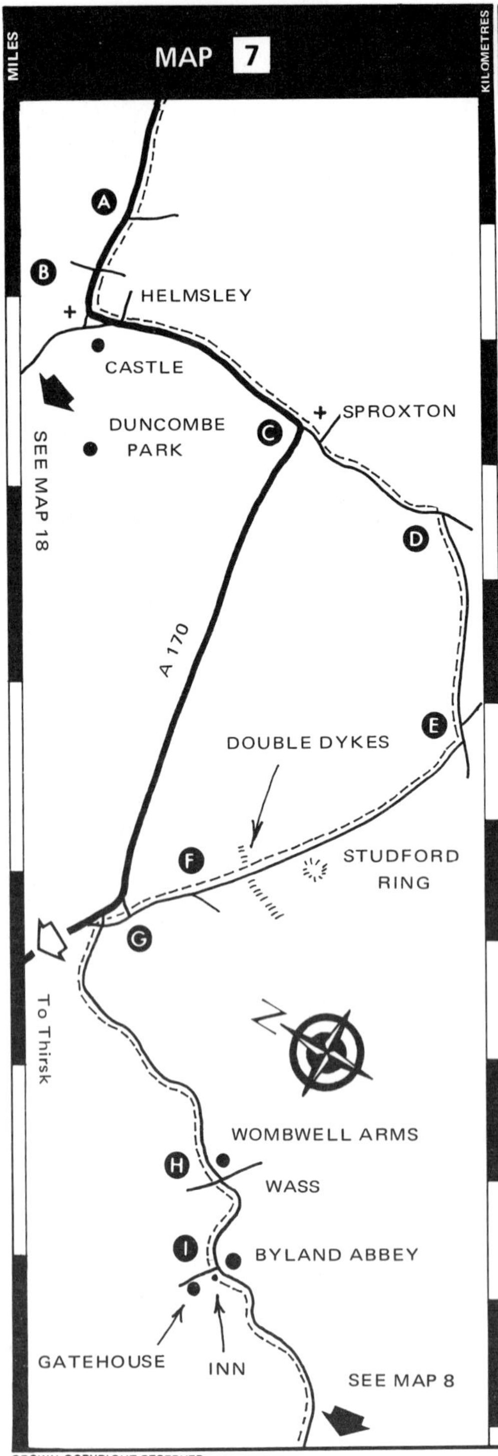

MAP 7

Map REF	Miles	DIRECTIONS FOR DRIVER	FOLLOW SIGN MARKED
A	.9	Straight, not left	Thirsk
	.3	Helmsley entry signed (Keep on A170 through Helmsley)	
	.1	Over small X rds.	Thirsk
B	.2	Turn left in Helmsley Market Square (BUT GO STRAIGHT AHEAD IF YOU WISH TO MOVE ON TO MAP 18, WHICH STARTS HERE) (Please park in Square if you wish to visit Castle)	Thirsk
	.1	Straight, not right, and...	No sign
		Straight, not left, and...	Thirsk
		Over bridge crossing River Rye	
C	1.2	Fork left, on to B1257 by Duncombe Park gates in Sproxton	Malton
	.1	Straight, not left, by church	No sign
D	.9	Turn right at T junction into woodlands	Ampleforth
E	1.1	Straight, not left, at Y junction	Ampleforth
	.1	Fork right at T junction	Thirsk
	.6	Pry Rigg woods on right	
	.4	Studford Ring over to left	
	.4	The Double Dykes cross our road here (not very evident)	
F	.3	Straight, not left, at Y junction	No sign
		Woods now on left	
G	.4	Straight, not right	No sign
	.1	Turn left at X rds.	Wass
		Woods now on both sides of road	
	.8	Steep Hill signed	
	.2	Down steep hill, into pleasant wooded valley	
	.7	Wass entry signed	
H	.1	Over X rds. by the Wombwell Arms, on to wider road	Byland Abbey
	.4	Byland Abbey entry signed, and...	
		Abbey on left	
I	.1	Bear left by the Abbey Inn (Abbey Gatehouse visible up right)	Thirsk
		Total mileage on this map: 9.5	

PLACES OF INTEREST ON THE ROUTE

Helmsley

This is our favourite North Yorks market town, and in our view, the best inland centre for exploring the North York Moors. It has a spacious market square enriched by an old cross and an elaborate Victorian monument close beside it. These are overlooked on the west side by a handsome little 17th century style Town Hall... built in 1901, but already convincingly mellowed. On the north side stands the attractive and comfortable Black Swan Hotel (one of several pleasant hotels in Helmsley, spreading over two Georgian houses and a much older timbered building. The church which lies just beyond the Black Swan, was re-built in 1866, and is remembered by us chiefly for its enchanting peal of bells.

The castle is best approached on foot from the square (beyond the Town Hall), and is well worth visiting. It was established in the 12th century, but the earliest remains date from the early 13th. A smoothly mown, double ditch surrounds the ruined curtain walls, gateways, towers, domestic buildings and dramatic ruined keep... the latter dominating everything most effectively.

From here are pleasant views out over Duncombe Park, a splendidly landscaped area surrounding a mansion which is attributed to Vanbrugh. This is now a school, but it is possible to walk on the long Terrace*, with its two 18th century temples. (Open: May – August, Wednesdays only 10 – 4).

See page 31 for THE CLEVELAND WAY, one end of which is at Helmsley.

*Not to be confused with Rievaulx Terrace (see p. 37).

Sproxton

A small village containing a neat little 17th century church, which was moved here from nearby West Newton Grange, and re-built in 1879. It has a stylish interior with 17th century screen and panelling, and a black marble font. The nearby entrance to Duncombe Park is in the form of a triumphal arch, and was erected in 1806 to commemorate Trafalgar.

Studford Ring and The Double Dykes

Earthworks close to our route (see Route Directions), both of which were probably thrown up in the Bronze Age for defensive purposes. Neither appear to us to be of much interest.

Wass

Pleasant hamlet at the bottom of a wooded valley, with flower filled cottage gardens, and a hospitable inn, the Wombwell Arms.

Byland Abbey

It was in 1177, after several unfortunate moves, that a Cistercian community finally settled here. However, once established, they built a magnificent church, larger than either Rievaulx or Fountains. This building, with its dramatically broken circle of a rose window in the west front, its extensive range of monastic quarters, and small isolated gatehouse, all in a wide quiet valley, is a delight to the eye, and should not on any account be missed.

1. Helmsley Castle

2. Rye Bridge, Helmsley

3. The Square at Helmsley

4. Cross and Church at Helmsley

5. Byland Abbey

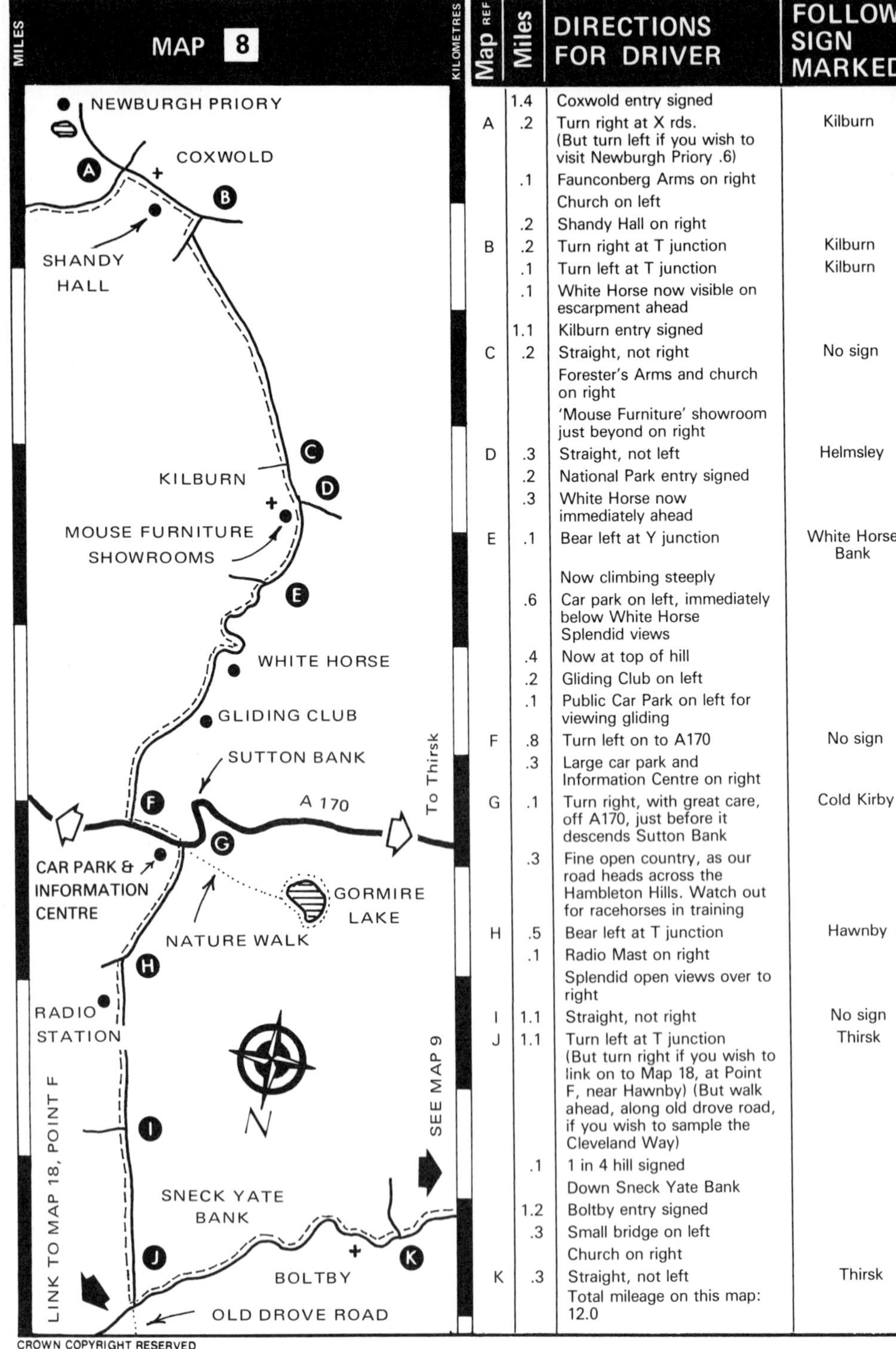

Map REF	Miles	DIRECTIONS FOR DRIVER	FOLLOW SIGN MARKED
	1.4	Coxwold entry signed	
A	.2	Turn right at X rds. (But turn left if you wish to visit Newburgh Priory .6)	Kilburn
	.1	Fauconberg Arms on right	
		Church on left	
	.2	Shandy Hall on right	
B	.2	Turn right at T junction	Kilburn
	.1	Turn left at T junction	Kilburn
	.1	White Horse now visible on escarpment ahead	
	1.1	Kilburn entry signed	
C	.2	Straight, not right	No sign
		Forester's Arms and church on right	
		'Mouse Furniture' showroom just beyond on right	
D	.3	Straight, not left	Helmsley
	.2	National Park entry signed	
	.3	White Horse now immediately ahead	
E	.1	Bear left at Y junction	White Horse Bank
		Now climbing steeply	
	.6	Car park on left, immediately below White Horse Splendid views	
	.4	Now at top of hill	
	.2	Gliding Club on left	
	.1	Public Car Park on left for viewing gliding	
F	.8	Turn left on to A170	No sign
	.3	Large car park and Information Centre on right	
G	.1	Turn right, with great care, off A170, just before it descends Sutton Bank	Cold Kirby
	.3	Fine open country, as our road heads across the Hambleton Hills. Watch out for racehorses in training	
H	.5	Bear left at T junction	Hawnby
	.1	Radio Mast on right	
		Splendid open views over to right	
I	1.1	Straight, not right	No sign
J	1.1	Turn left at T junction (But turn right if you wish to link on to Map 18, at Point F, near Hawnby) (But walk ahead, along old drove road, if you wish to sample the Cleveland Way)	Thirsk
	.1	1 in 4 hill signed	
		Down Sneck Yate Bank	
	1.2	Boltby entry signed	
	.3	Small bridge on left	
		Church on right	
K	.3	Straight, not left	Thirsk
		Total mileage on this map: 12.0	

PLACES OF INTEREST ON THE ROUTE

Newburgh Priory

A good looking, largely 17th and 18th century mansion, on the site of an Augustinian Priory, established here in the 12th century. We particularly liked the elegant wrought iron gates and the early Georgian stable block, with pavilions at two ends.

Coxwold

A thoroughly pleasing village, probably the most attractive in the North York Moors area, but still remarkably unspoilt. The single village street rises up from a crossroads towards the octagonal towered church, passing wide grass verges, and a variety of trim stone cottages. See especially the charming Fauconberg Arms, the Fauconberg Hospital (almshouses), the 17th century Grammar School, Colville Hall by the church, and the delightful church itself. This has a fascinating interior, with box pews, two decker pulpit, and a series of lovely monuments in the chancel.

Shandy Hall

Laurence Sterne lived at Coxwold for the last eight years of his life (1760 – 8), and named his house after the hero of his novel 'The Life and Opinions of Tristram Shandy'. Shandy Hall is a long low, mellow brick building, and has been lovingly restored as a museum by the Sterne Trust.

Kilburn

Lies beneath the steep slopes of the Hambleton Hills, here embellished with a massive White Horse, cut in the hillside in 1857. A stream runs beside the village street and the church (Norman origins) looks out over a small space between the bright and cheerful Forester's Arms and the little school.

However most visitors to Kilburn are more interested in the furniture workshops established here by Robert Thompson (1876 – 1955). His world famous 'signature' of a carved mouse upon each piece can be found in over seven hundred churches, including Westminster Abbey and York Minster. The tradition is carried on by his grandsons and their team of craftsmen, who continue to produce robust oak furniture, complete of course, with a mouse upon each piece. The showroom is usually open, and permission to look round the most interesting workshops can usually be obtained.

Sutton Bank

The large car park (with Information Centre) above this long steep hill (not on our route) is a popular stopping place for visitors. There are fine views south to Roulston Scar, and westwards out over the Vale of York, and there is a Nature Trail leading down to, and around, the beautiful Gormire Lake.

Hambleton Hills

Our route, here following the line of the Old Drove Road, takes us across the windy downland tops of these hills. This is an area much used for the exercising of race horses... PLEASE DRIVE WITH CARE.

Link to Hawnby (see page 19)

Boltby (see page 19)

1. Spring Morning at Coxwold

2. Shandy Hall, Coxwold

3. Kilburn Church

4. Sneck Yate Bank

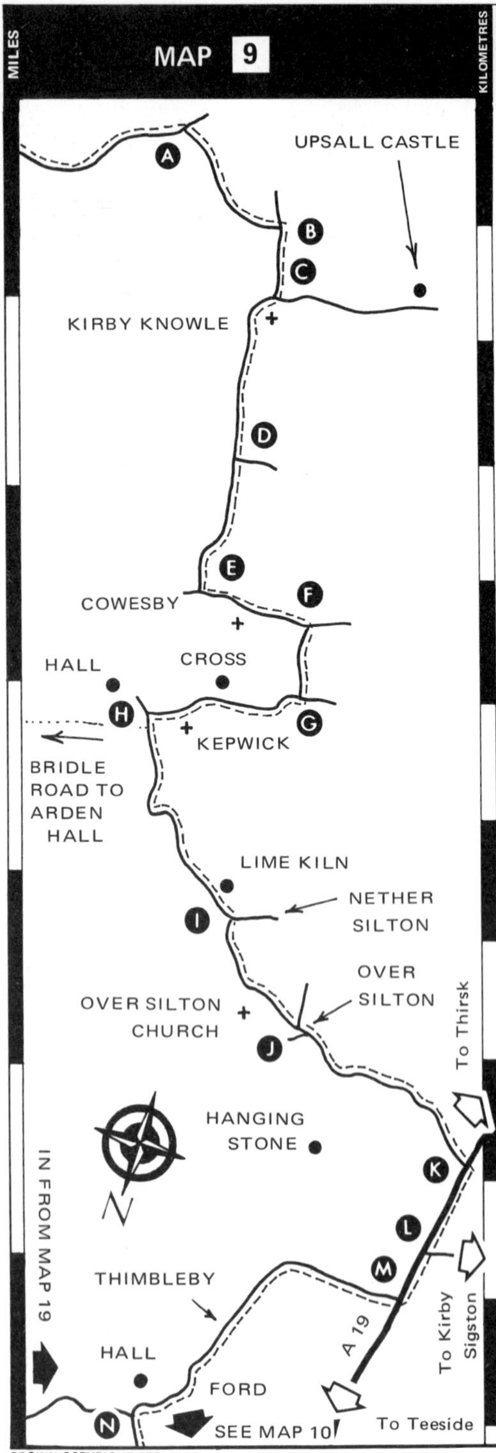

MAP 9

Map REF	Miles	DIRECTIONS FOR DRIVER	FOLLOW SIGN MARKED
	.2	Fine views of Sutton Bank back left	
A	.4	Turn right at T junction	Kirby Knowle
	.3	Pleasant road with bracken covered hillside to right	
B	.5	Turn right at T junction	Kirby Knowle
	.1	Kirby Knowle entry signed	
	.1	Views of Upsall Castle over to left	
C	.2	Turn right at T junction	Cowesby
		Church on left	
	.1	Turn left at T junction	Cowesby
	.5	Into woodlands	
D	.3	Straight, not left	Cowesby
	.8	Cowesby entry signed	
E	.2	Turn left by phone box	Kepwick
		Almshouses on right	
	.1	Church on right	
F	.3	Turn right at T junction	Kepwick
G	.5	Turn right at T junction	Kepwick
		Small monument on hill to right	
	.4	Kepwick entry signed	
	.2	Church on left	
H	.2	Bear left at T junction by gates to Kepwick Hall (Bridle road to Arden Hall on right, see p. 37)	Silton
	1.1	Old lime kiln visible to left	
I	.2	Turn right at T junction	Over Silton
	.1	Fork left just beyond cottage	No sign
	.4	Over Silton church, over to right, in field	
J	.3	Straight, not left, by Over Silton entry sign, and...	Northallerton
		Bear left at T junction (Bridle way to Thimbleby up right)	Osmotherley
	.3	The Hanging Stone well over to right (rocky bluff)	
K	1.1	Turn right, with great care, on to A19	Teeside
L	.5	Straight, not left, keeping on A19 by the Haynes Arms Inn	Teeside
M	.3	Turn right, off A19	Thimbleby
	.7	Thimbleby entry signed	
	.8	Gates to Thimbleby Hall on right	
	.3	Through ford	
N	.2	Straight, not right, at entry to Osmotherley (WE ARE JOINED HERE FROM THE END OF MAP 19)	Osmotherley
		Total mileage on this map: 11.7	

PLACES OF INTEREST ON THE ROUTE

Link to Hawnby (see page 16)

See Route Directions (Map 8) and Key Map, if you wish to link on to Map 18 at Point F, near Hawnby, on an attractive road down a wooded valley... about 3 miles.

Boltby (see page 16)

A pleasant, but unexceptional village below Sneck Yate Bank, with a Victorian chapel, and a little stone bridge.

Kirby Knowle

Shelters beneath the high moorland edge to its east, with a Victorian church. Inside there is a lectern carved by Robert Thompson of Kilburn, complete with mouse (see page 17).

Cowesby

A sleepy village backed by the high moors, complete with a row of 17th century almshouses, with climbing roses everywhere; and a rather unusual church. This lies in an overgrown churchyard, with a long avenue of trees leading to the south door. This opens on to a stylish interior, typical of the Victorian architect, Anthony Salvin, who rebuilt the church in the neo-Norman style in 1846. We particularly liked the detail in the chancel and tower arches, and the impressive 'Commandment Boards'.

Kepwick

There is a small Victorian monument (a 'broken' column) in a clump of trees to our right, just before entering this pretty village beneath bracken covered hillsides. There is a small Victorian chapel, and rows of cottages, with flower filled gardens looking out onto wide grass verges, especially spacious near the entrance gates to Kepwick Hall. There is a bridle road over the moors to Arden Hall (see page 37), which starts to our right, immediately beyond Kepwick Hall gates... about three miles.

Over Silton Church

The hamlet of Over Silton is not exceptional, but the little church is delightfully sited in fields some distance from the road. Its churchyard was bright with daffodils when we called, and the church, in honey coloured stone, with small bellcote and little Norman doorway, reminded us strongly of the Cotswolds. Its interior has been disappointingly restored, with undistinguished pews and shiny tiles... but this charming little building is still worth the walk over from the road.

The Hanging Stone

This is a dramatically poised portion of rock, almost broken away from the main rock-face, and is just visible over to the right, from our road beyond Over Silton. However it is best viewed from the bridleway which runs from Over Silton to Thimbleby.

Thimbleby

A hamlet with pleasant 18th century houses and cottages, and a mansion of the same period, which is not visible from the road... this is Thimbleby Hall. The lodge and gates provide us with an impression of the elegance within the park.

1. Our Road Beyond Boltby

2. and 3. Daffodils at Over Silton

4. Gateway to Thimbleby Hall

5. Waterfall at Thimbleby Ford

MAP 10

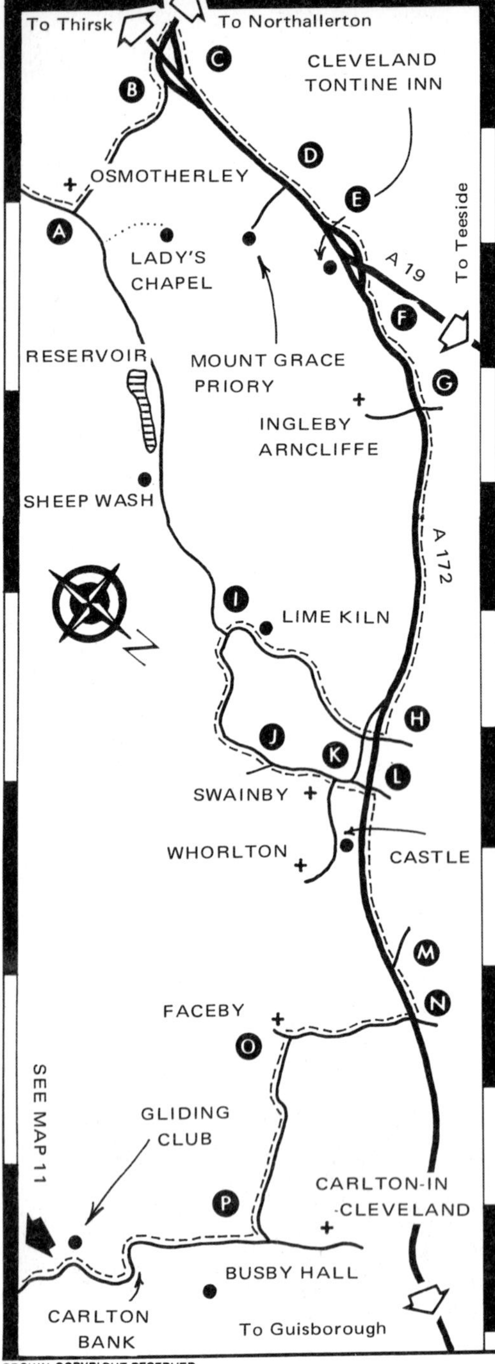

Map ref	Miles	DIRECTIONS FOR DRIVER	FOLLOW SIGN MARKED
A	.3	Turn left by the Queen Catherine Inn (But go straight ahead for .3 and walk up left, and then fork right if you wish to visit the 'Lady's Chapel')	Northallerton
B	.9	Turn left, on to main road by the King's Head	Teeside
	.1	Under bridge beneath A19, and...	
	.2	Turn right, on to A19 approach road, and...	Teeside
C	.3	Bear left, with care, on to A19	Teeside
D	.9	Straight, not right, keeping on A19 (But turn right if you wish to visit Mount Grace Priory... .4)	No sign
	.1	Straight, not left	Stokesley
E	.3	Bear left, off A19, on to A172, by the Cleveland Tontine Inn	Stokesley
F	.5	Straight, not right	Middlesborough
	.5	Ingleby Cross signed	
G	.1	Over X rds. by the Blue Bell Inn (But turn right if you wish to visit Ingleby Arncliffe church... .4)	Middlesborough
H	1.8	Turn right, off A172 and immediately...	Swainby
		Over 2nd X rds.	Snilesworth
I	1.2	Bear left at T junction on hill	No sign
J	1.0	Straight, not right, at entry to Swainby	No sign
K	.3	Straight, not right by 'new' church and bridge (But turn right if you wish to visit Whorlton Castle and Whorlton 'old' church... .5)	No sign
	.1	Turn right over bridge by the Blacksmith's Arms, and immediately...	
		Turn left	Stokesley
L	.1	Turn right, on to A172	Stokesley
M	1.0	Straight, not left, keeping on A172	No sign
N	.2	Turn right at X rds., off A172	Faceby
	.5	Faceby entry signed	
O	.2	Bear left, at T junction by the Sutton Arms	Carlton
	.3	Over 'dry' ford	
	.5	Carlton-in-Cleveland entry signed	
P	.3	Turn sharp right (But turn left if you wish to visit village)	Chop Gate
	.8	Climb steeply up Carlton Bank	
	.3	Splendid views over to left, of Roseberry Topping	
	.3	Entrance to Gliding Club on right	
		Total mileage on this map: 13.1	

PLACES OF INTEREST ON THE ROUTE

Osmotherley (see page 39)

Lady's Chapel (see Route Directions)

Built in the early 16th century by the Prior of Mount Grace, this remained a place of pilgrimage long after the Reformation. It has been extensively restored, but is still well worth a visit, especially for its splendid views out over the plain.

Mount Grace Priory

Delightfully set below steep wooded hillsides, Mount Grace is perhaps the best surviving example of a Carthusian foundation in Britain. The complex layout of the monastic quarters was governed by the necessity for each brother to remain largely isolated from his fellows, a peculiarity of the Carthusian Order. The ruined church, the gatehouse and the guest house (later converted into a private house) complete a most interesting group of buildings.

The Cleveland Tontine Inn

A famous coaching inn, built in 1804 to serve a new turnpike road. A TONTINE is 'a form of joint annuity whereby the sum received by subscribers increases as their number decreases, until with the death of the last subscriber the tontine completely lapses'... it is named after a certain Lorenzo Tonti, a 17th century Italian who dreamed up the idea.

Ingleby Arncliffe

We liked the early 19th century church, with its interior all contemporary with the building... box pews, three decker pulpit and ship model... all rather reminiscent of Fylingthorpe Old Church (see page 3). The church lies just below the handsome Arncliffe Hall, designed by the famous John Carr of York in the 1750's, and both buildings are enriched by their quiet setting beneath wooded hillsides.

Swainby

Is neatly situated on either side of the Scugdale Beck, with grassy banks and stone bridges... a spacious place with a very pleasing atmosphere. The church is Victorian and unexceptional, but the Blacksmith's Arms has a curious collection of walking sticks displayed upon its walls.

Whorlton

Life has now moved down into Swainby, but its partially ruined church is full of atmosphere, and a 14th century effigy is visible in the still roofed chancel. Whorlton Castle is well sited above the plain, but the gate house is the only significant structure remaining.

Carlton-in-Cleveland

A most agreeable village, with houses looking across at each other above a stream in a miniature valley. It is complete with a smithy, still in active use, a pleasant pub, The Blackwell Ox, a handsome Palladian style manor house, and a miniature ford. The church is not of great interest to visitors.

Carlton Bank

A steep climb up on to the moors, with fine views out over the plain, and to the charmingly titled conical hill of Roseberry Topping. There is gliding near here.

1. Snow and Daffodils at Mount Grace

2. Mount Grace Priory

3. Stream at Swainby

4. Whorlton Castle

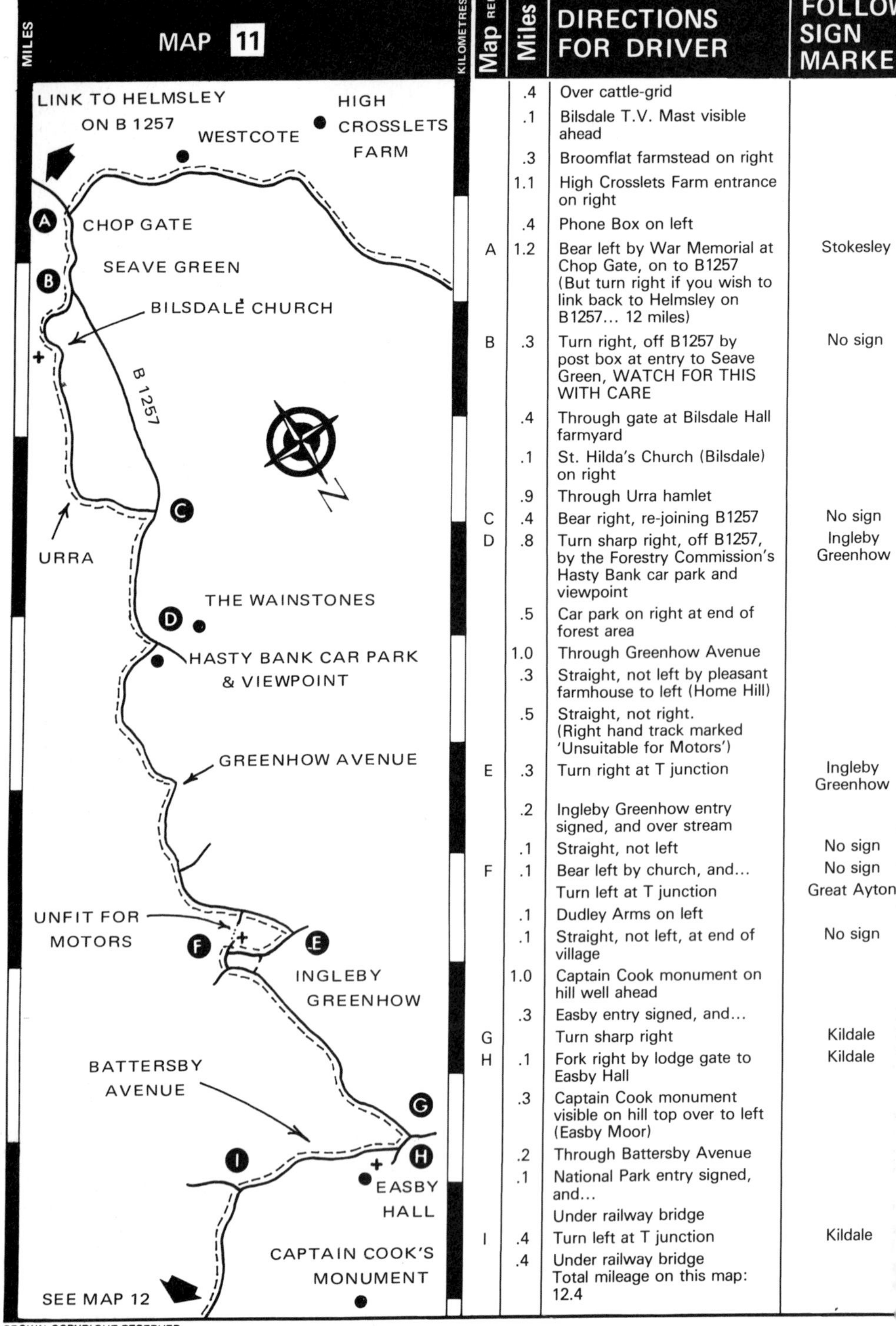

Map REF	Miles	DIRECTIONS FOR DRIVER	FOLLOW SIGN MARKED
	.4	Over cattle-grid	
	.1	Bilsdale T.V. Mast visible ahead	
	.3	Broomflat farmstead on right	
	1.1	High Crosslets Farm entrance on right	
	.4	Phone Box on left	
A	1.2	Bear left by War Memorial at Chop Gate, on to B1257 (But turn right if you wish to link back to Helmsley on B1257... 12 miles)	Stokesley
B	.3	Turn right, off B1257 by post box at entry to Seave Green, WATCH FOR THIS WITH CARE	No sign
	.4	Through gate at Bilsdale Hall farmyard	
	.1	St. Hilda's Church (Bilsdale) on right	
	.9	Through Urra hamlet	
C	.4	Bear right, re-joining B1257	No sign
D	.8	Turn sharp right, off B1257, by the Forestry Commission's Hasty Bank car park and viewpoint	Ingleby Greenhow
	.5	Car park on right at end of forest area	
	1.0	Through Greenhow Avenue	
	.3	Straight, not left by pleasant farmhouse to left (Home Hill)	
	.5	Straight, not right. (Right hand track marked 'Unsuitable for Motors')	
E	.3	Turn right at T junction	Ingleby Greenhow
	.2	Ingleby Greenhow entry signed, and over stream	
	.1	Straight, not left	No sign
F	.1	Bear left by church, and...	No sign
		Turn left at T junction	Great Ayton
	.1	Dudley Arms on left	
	.1	Straight, not left, at end of village	No sign
	1.0	Captain Cook monument on hill well ahead	
	.3	Easby entry signed, and...	
G		Turn sharp right	Kildale
H	.1	Fork right by lodge gate to Easby Hall	Kildale
	.3	Captain Cook monument visible on hill top over to left (Easby Moor)	
	.2	Through Battersby Avenue	
	.1	National Park entry signed, and...	
		Under railway bridge	
I	.4	Turn left at T junction	Kildale
	.4	Under railway bridge Total mileage on this map: 12.4	

PLACES OF INTEREST ON THE ROUTE

Raisdale

We soon drop into upper Raisdale beyond Carlton Bank, but for some time there are fine views over Snilesworth and Bilsdale Moors... ahead right.

Chop Gate

Pronounced Chop Yat locally, this is a pleasant hamlet at the junction of Raisdale and Bilsdale, and has a petrol station, an inn, a shop and a Wesleyan chapel. Turn right here on to the B1257, if you wish to return to Helmsley by driving south down Bilsdale... about twelve miles.

Bilsdale Church

This is rather an unexciting Victorian building, with a small bellcote. Nearby Bilsdale Hall Farm is more attractive... please drive quietly through the farmyard area, and close gates where necessary.

Hasty Bank and The Wainstones

The Forestry Commission has provided a good car park, and there are panoramic views out across woodlands to the Cleveland Hills, Baysdale Moor, Roseberry Topping and the Cook Monument on Easby Moor. Cross the B1257 from the car park and walk up westwards to visit THE WAINSTONES, a series of rocky tor-like outcrops on the upper slopes of Hasty Bank. Refer to map displayed at car park for details.

Greenhow Avenue

On our road to Ingleby Greenhow we pass along Greenhow Avenue... 'planted in 1965 as thanksgiving to God for the deliverance of this country in two world wars'... What a pleasant idea.

Ingleby Greenhow

The church overlooks a ford and footbridge over the little Ingleby Beck. It has a minute tower and was largely re-built in the 18th century. However the interior contains several Norman features, including the chancel arch and the arcading, the latter with amusingly primitive men and beasts.

Easby

A small hamlet with Forge Cottage and the little Methodist chapel harmonising well together. The Victorian chapel beyond the lodge is private.

Captain Cook Monument

Turn left at Point G, turn right three times through Little Ayton, and then drive beyond Ayton Railway Halt, for the easiest access to the Captain Cook Monument, which stands above us on Easby Moor. However see page 25 for alternative access from Kildale.

Captain Cook was born at Marton, went to school at Great Ayton, (both a few miles to the north) and was apprenticed at Staithes (see page 27).

Snever Dale Forest Trail (see page 6)

This is an interesting three mile trail waymarked with red fox heads (shortened version 1¾ miles), starting from our route within the Dalby Forest Drive. If leaflets are not available at the starting point, drive about half a mile to the Information Centre at Low Dalby.

1. Carlton Bank (see page 20)

2. Snow in Raisdale

3. Viewpoint at Hasty Bank

4. Ingleby Greenhow

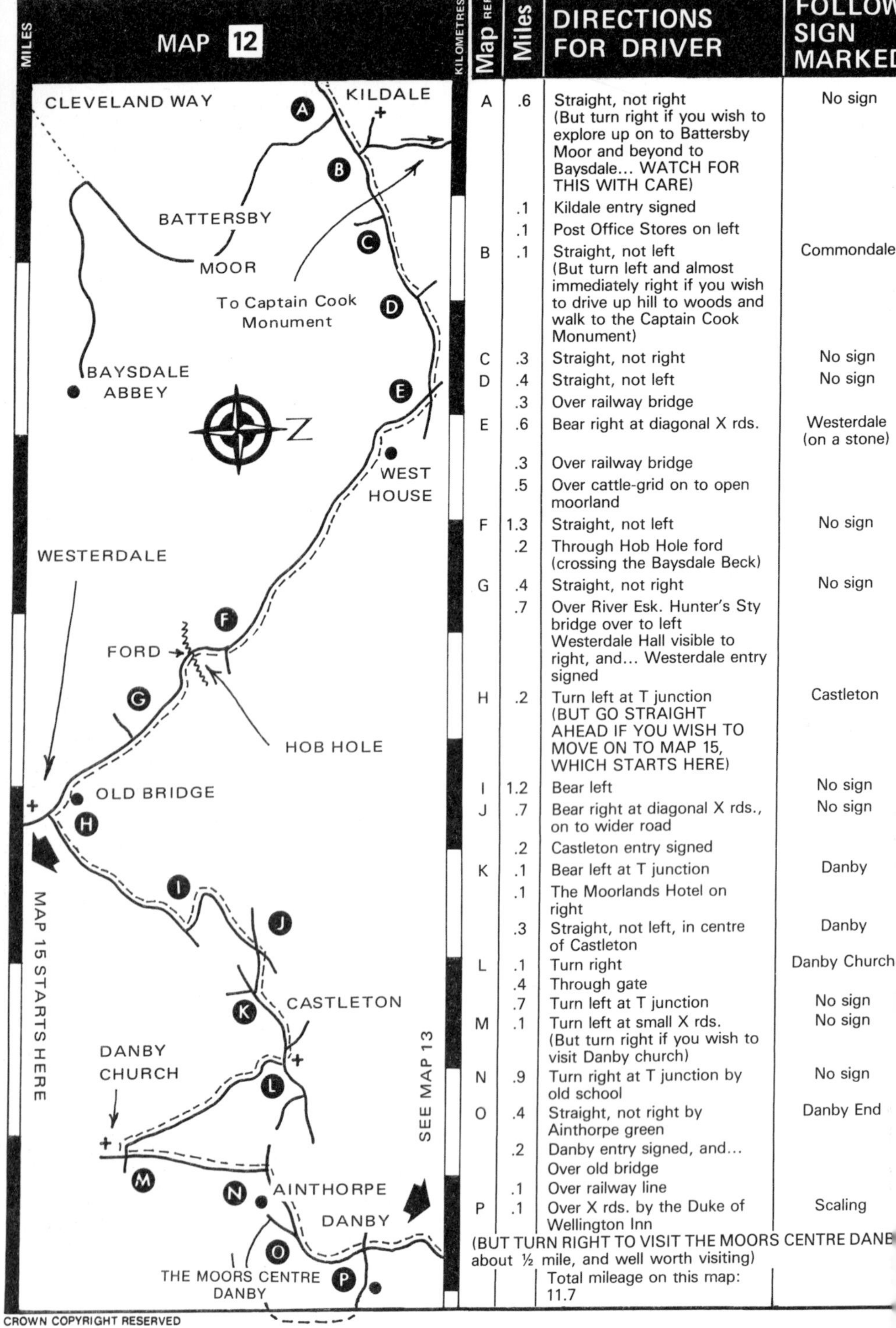

Map REF	Miles	DIRECTIONS FOR DRIVER	FOLLOW SIGN MARKED
A	.6	Straight, not right (But turn right if you wish to explore up on to Battersby Moor and beyond to Baysdale... WATCH FOR THIS WITH CARE)	No sign
	.1	Kildale entry signed	
	.1	Post Office Stores on left	
B	.1	Straight, not left (But turn left and almost immediately right if you wish to drive up hill to woods and walk to the Captain Cook Monument)	Commondale
C	.3	Straight, not right	No sign
D	.4	Straight, not left	No sign
	.3	Over railway bridge	
E	.6	Bear right at diagonal X rds.	Westerdale (on a stone)
	.3	Over railway bridge	
	.5	Over cattle-grid on to open moorland	
F	1.3	Straight, not left	No sign
	.2	Through Hob Hole ford (crossing the Baysdale Beck)	
G	.4	Straight, not right	No sign
	.7	Over River Esk. Hunter's Sty bridge over to left Westerdale Hall visible to right, and... Westerdale entry signed	
H	.2	Turn left at T junction (BUT GO STRAIGHT AHEAD IF YOU WISH TO MOVE ON TO MAP 15, WHICH STARTS HERE)	Castleton
I	1.2	Bear left	No sign
J	.7	Bear right at diagonal X rds., on to wider road	No sign
	.2	Castleton entry signed	
K	.1	Bear left at T junction	Danby
	.1	The Moorlands Hotel on right	
	.3	Straight, not left, in centre of Castleton	Danby
L	.1	Turn right	Danby Church
	.4	Through gate	
	.7	Turn left at T junction	No sign
M	.1	Turn left at small X rds. (But turn right if you wish to visit Danby church)	No sign
N	.9	Turn right at T junction by old school	No sign
O	.4	Straight, not right by Ainthorpe green	Danby End
	.2	Danby entry signed, and... Over old bridge	
	.1	Over railway line	
P	.1	Over X rds. by the Duke of Wellington Inn	Scaling
(BUT TURN RIGHT TO VISIT THE MOORS CENTRE DANB about ½ mile, and well worth visiting)			
		Total mileage on this map: 11.7	

PLACES OF INTEREST ON THE ROUTE

Diversion to Battersby Moor and Baysdale

Watch for this diversion, and turn right at Point A, following a sign marked NO THROUGH ROAD, and a sign marked MOORS PATH, the latter indicating that we are following the Cleveland Way (see page 39). Within 1.7 miles there are splendid views out over Kildale to the Captain Cook Monument and to Roseberry Topping. At 2 miles, the road along the top ends and the Cleveland Way stretches out into the distance. The road turns sharply to the left and descends into Baysdale, but we suggest that you stop at 2.2 and walk if you wish to explore down into Baysdale... for it is a valley that deserves tranquillity.

Kildale

Small village with a pretty little stone Post Office stores, dated 1782. The Victorian church has a Norman font, but little else of interest. The Percy family had a castle here, but the earthworks have been partially built over, and partially eaten into by the railway, and there is little of interest to be seen.

Follow diversion from Point B, and climb out of Kildale (by car) for one mile to arrive at the edge of woodland. Park here and follow track to left through woods for about a mile to reach the Captain Cook Monument on Easby Moor (see page 23).

Hob Hole

This is a local name for the place where our road fords the little Baysdale Beck. It seems a pity that the footbridge has to be so aggressively 'public-park- like', but this is still a delightful place to stop awhile... a deep valley surrounded by moorland, with a wide stretch of springy turf beside the stream.

Hunter's Sty Bridge, Westerdale

This must have been a most attractive medieval pack-horse bridge before it was so ruthlessly restored in 1874. However close inspection still reveals old vaulting beneath, and old slabs on the roadway.

Westerdale (see page 31)

Castleton

A rather indeterminate village, sprawling out over the upper Esk valley. The church was built in the 1920's in memory of the men of Castleton who died in the 14 – 18 War, and the many carved mice to be found signify the extent of Robert Thompson's contribution to the furnishing (see Kilburn, page 17). The castle earthworks lie to the west of the church, overlooking the Esk, but are of no great interest.

Danby Church

This is situated in a remote valley, looking up the broad Danby Dale towards Danby Moor. It is a large church, in a large churchyard, with a 15th century tower, a nave built in 1789, and a chancel in 1848. The end result is rather disappointing.

Danby Village and the Moors Centre

Apart from Ainthorpe hamlet (good stone building and small stream), we found Danby to be a scrappy

continued on page 27

1. Road Above Baysdale

2. Baysdale Beck at Hob Hole

3. Westerdale Bridge

4. War Memorial, Castleton

MAP 13

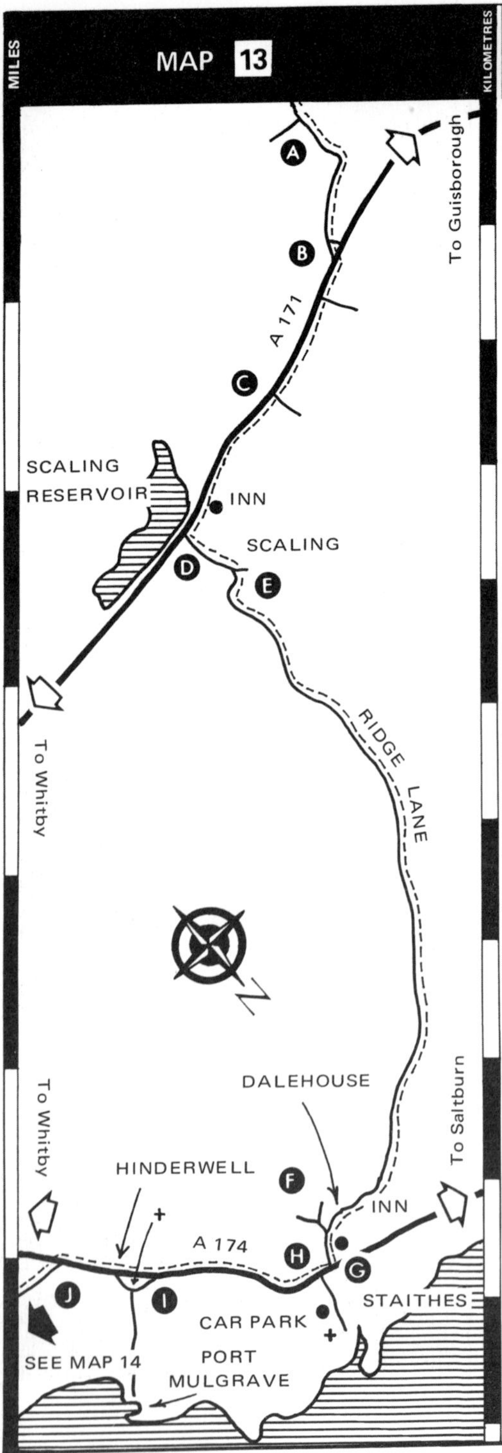

Map REF	Miles	DIRECTIONS FOR DRIVER	FOLLOW SIGN MARKED
A	1.1	Straight, not right	No sign
	.8	Bend sharp right	No sign
B	.6	Turn right, on to A171	Whitby
	.2	Straight, not left, keeping on A171	Whitby
C	.6	Straight, not left, keeping on A171	Whitby
		Sailing Club and reservoir on right	
	.6	Scaling Dam entry signed	
	.1	Bunch of Grapes Inn on left	
D	.2	Turn left, off A171, by Petrol Station	Scaling
	.3	Wesleyan Chapel on left	
E	.1	Fork right in Scaling hamlet by pleasant farmhouse	No sign
	.8	Now in Ridge Lane... a pleasantly wooded area	
	1.4	Small castellated lodge on left	
	.2	Large cement works visible ahead	
	.1	Sea visible ahead	
	1.2	Down steep hill	
	.2	Through 'dry' ford	
F	.3	Bear left, on to wider road, in Dalehouse hamlet	No sign
	.1	Straight, not left, by the Fox and Hounds	Staithes
G	.2	Turn right, with great care, on to A174	Whitby
H	.1	Straight, not left, keeping on A174 (But turn left, and drive .2 to car park, if you wish to explore Staithes... DON'T MISS IT)	Whitby
I	1.0	Straight, not left by Hinderwell Church (But turn left and left again behind church if you wish to visit Port Mulgrave... .7)	No sign
J	.5	Fork left, off A174, by War Memorial in Hinderwell	Runswick Bay
		Total mileage on this map: 10.7	

PLACES OF INTEREST ON THE ROUTE

Danby *continued from page 25*
place, with much 'between the wars' building. Danby Lodge, a former shooting lodge, is now The Moors Centre and is open every day from 10-6. Allow at least 2 hours for your visit to this most interesting Centre. Several walks emanate from here (leaflets available, and guided walks in the afternoons).

Scaling Reservoir

Pleasant stretch of water, with open moorland on three sides, and overlooked on the fourth by the hamlet of Scaling Dam, complete with cheerful inn, The Bunch of Grapes. Sailing dinghies are to be seen here at weekends.

Scaling

Small hamlet at the northern end of Ridge Lane, with a pleasant farmhouse, a Wesleyan chapel, and a 'craft shop'.

Ridge Lane

A narrow, but most enchanting road through woodlands, covering a ridge between two steep sided valleys. Drive carefully.

Dalehouse

Quiet hamlet in a deep valley to the immediate south of the A174, and only a stones throw away from bustling Staithes. We liked the Fox and Hounds... a character inn, with real North Country flavour.

Staithes

(Do not attempt to take your car down to Staithes, but use the Car Park as directed, even at quiet times of the year.)

Salty little fishing port, with stream flowing out between high cliffs. Despite severe damage inflicted by storms over the centuries, Staithes still survives; although its heyday as a centre for mackerel, haddock and cod has long since passed (harbour far too small for modern trawlers). Captain Cook was apprenticed here to a grocer in 1745, but in the following year, joined a ship sailing out of Whitby.

Staithes has some superficial resemblance to Polperro, but with its cobbled streets, its great cliffs and small fishing boats, it has a tougher, more genuine flavour. Perhaps we saw it at its best... with sun breaking through after dark storms in early April.

Hinderwell

Large village stretching along either side of the A174, with two inns, The Brown Cow and The Badger Hound, and an 18th and 19th century church. This has a good 19th century gallery and a not very inspiring Holy Well, in the churchyard (St. Hild's Well... hence Hinderwell).

Port Mulgrave

Park at the far end of the road (very small car park space), and walk onwards with great care to explore the remains of this little harbour, once used for the shipping of ironstone from mines inland, with which it was connected by a mile long tunnel. For those who don't wish to walk, there are splendid cliff views south eastwards.

1. The Moors Centre, Danby

2. After The Storm — Staithes

3. High Tide at Staithes

4. Cliff View, Above Port Mulgrave

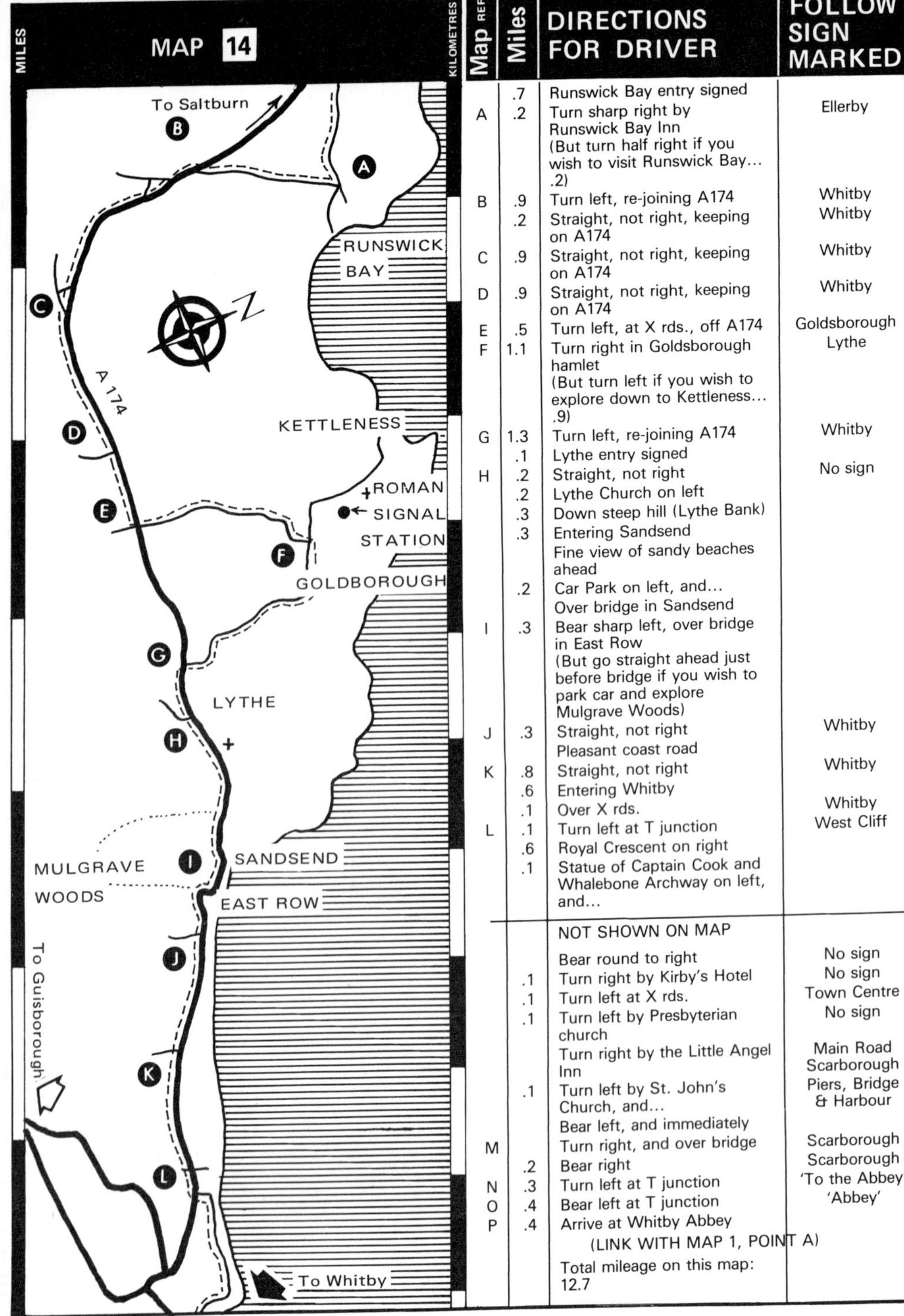

Map Ref	Miles	DIRECTIONS FOR DRIVER	FOLLOW SIGN MARKED
	.7	Runswick Bay entry signed	
A	.2	Turn sharp right by Runswick Bay Inn (But turn half right if you wish to visit Runswick Bay... .2)	Ellerby
B	.9	Turn left, re-joining A174	Whitby
	.2	Straight, not right, keeping on A174	Whitby
C	.9	Straight, not right, keeping on A174	Whitby
D	.9	Straight, not right, keeping on A174	Whitby
E	.5	Turn left, at X rds., off A174	Goldsborough
F	1.1	Turn right in Goldsborough hamlet (But turn left if you wish to explore down to Kettleness... .9)	Lythe
G	1.3	Turn left, re-joining A174	Whitby
	.1	Lythe entry signed	
H	.2	Straight, not right	No sign
	.2	Lythe Church on left	
	.3	Down steep hill (Lythe Bank)	
	.3	Entering Sandsend	
		Fine view of sandy beaches ahead	
	.2	Car Park on left, and...	
		Over bridge in Sandsend	
I	.3	Bear sharp left, over bridge in East Row (But go straight ahead just before bridge if you wish to park car and explore Mulgrave Woods)	
J	.3	Straight, not right	Whitby
		Pleasant coast road	
K	.8	Straight, not right	Whitby
	.6	Entering Whitby	
	.1	Over X rds.	Whitby
L	.1	Turn left at T junction	West Cliff
	.6	Royal Crescent on right	
	.1	Statue of Captain Cook and Whalebone Archway on left, and...	
		NOT SHOWN ON MAP	
		Bear round to right	No sign
	.1	Turn right by Kirby's Hotel	No sign
	.1	Turn left at X rds.	Town Centre
	.1	Turn left by Presbyterian church	No sign
		Turn right by the Little Angel Inn	Main Road Scarborough
	.1	Turn left by St. John's Church, and...	Piers, Bridge & Harbour
		Bear left, and immediately	
M		Turn right, and over bridge	Scarborough
	.2	Bear right	Scarborough
N	.3	Turn left at T junction	'To the Abbey'
O	.4	Bear left at T junction	'Abbey'
P	.4	Arrive at Whitby Abbey	

(LINK WITH MAP 1, POINT A)

Total mileage on this map: 12.7

PLACES OF INTEREST ON THE ROUTE

Runswick

Small fishing village perched precariously at the western end of cliff-encompassed, Runswick Bay, with fine views across to Kettle Ness, the eastern point of the Bay. There are attractive cottages, flower filled gardens, and small winding alleys and pathways... all part of a village, which replaced an earlier one that appears to have slipped into the sea in entirety in the year 1682. There is a good car park, a lifeboat station, and a beautiful stretch of sand.

Goldsborough

Small, completely unspoilt hamlet, just inland from the coastal cliffs, with a minute inn called the Fox and Hounds. A Roman Signal Station was excavated here in 1919, but its site lies well over to the right of our road, and is not accessible.

Kettleness

Most of this village was washed away in a storm in 1829, but inland of the old coastguard cottages lies the re-used remains of a railway station... a period piece exhibiting Victorian architecture at its very worst. However be not dismayed... there is appetizing coastal scenery and a cliff path all the way south eastwards to Sandsend (see below). (This is part of the Cleveland Way... see page 39).

Lythe

An agreeable little village astride the busy A174, with tidy stone houses, shops and an inn. The church stands well beyond the village in a windswept churchyard overlooking the sea. It was virtually rebuilt in 1910 and has a fine west tower, topped by a short stone spire. It has an ambitious interior with much stone vaulting, but most visitors come here to look at the interesting fragments of Anglo-Saxon and Anglo-Danish sculpture. Also do not miss the two ophicleides... '18th century wind instruments used to support the choir'.

Sandsend and East Row

Village at the western end of the Sandsend Bay (or more properly... Sandsend Wyke). There is a sandy beach with some shingle. East Row has some pleasant Georgian houses and cottages overlooking a stream flowing beneath an old stone bridge, and on to the sands. From the car park here, it is possible to walk up through Mulgrave Woods as far as the remains of the Old Mulgrave Castle, and back down a parallel valley to join the A174 at Lythe Bank. (This is part of the Mulgrave Estate, and is only open to pedestrians on Wednesdays, Saturdays and Sundays, except in May when it is closed entirely.)

1. Cottage at Runswick

2. Sandsend Bay

3. Whitby Harbour

4. Whitby Abbey

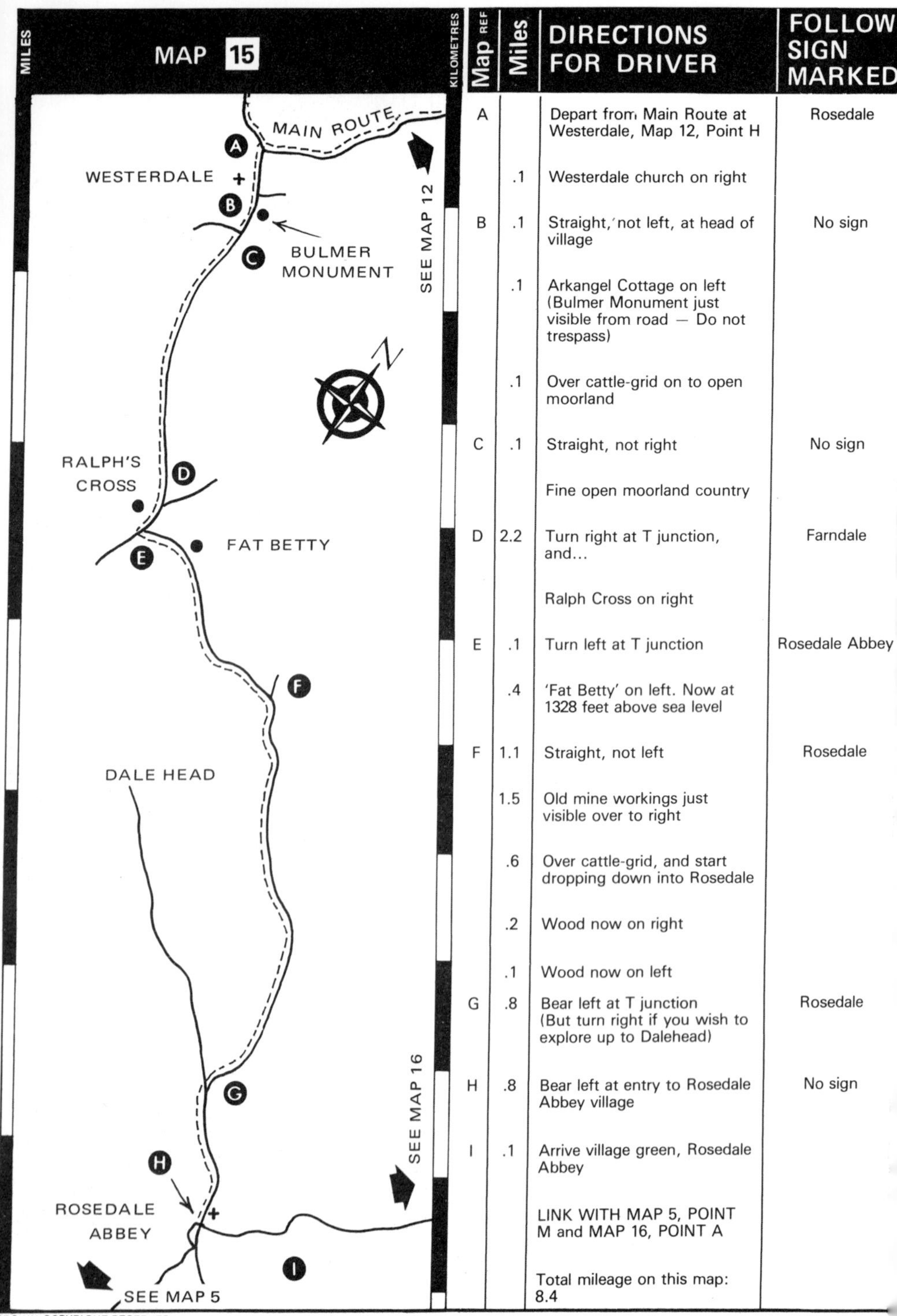

Map REF	Miles	DIRECTIONS FOR DRIVER	FOLLOW SIGN MARKED
A		Depart from Main Route at Westerdale, Map 12, Point H	Rosedale
	.1	Westerdale church on right	
B	.1	Straight, not left, at head of village	No sign
	.1	Arkangel Cottage on left (Bulmer Monument just visible from road — Do not trespass)	
	.1	Over cattle-grid on to open moorland	
C	.1	Straight, not right	No sign
		Fine open moorland country	
D	2.2	Turn right at T junction, and...	Farndale
		Ralph Cross on right	
E	.1	Turn left at T junction	Rosedale Abbey
	.4	'Fat Betty' on left. Now at 1328 feet above sea level	
F	1.1	Straight, not left	Rosedale
	1.5	Old mine workings just visible over to right	
	.6	Over cattle-grid, and start dropping down into Rosedale	
	.2	Wood now on right	
	.1	Wood now on left	
G	.8	Bear left at T junction (But turn right if you wish to explore up to Dalehead)	Rosedale
H	.8	Bear left at entry to Rosedale Abbey village	No sign
I	.1	Arrive village green, Rosedale Abbey	
		LINK WITH MAP 5, POINT M and MAP 16, POINT A	
		Total mileage on this map: 8.4	

PLACES OF INTEREST ON THE ROUTE

Westerdale

Lies above the upper reaches of the Esk, almost entirely surrounded by high moorland. We first came this way in early April with snow lying on the moors, and the tower of Westerdale Hall stood out most romantically in the low afternoon sunlight, as if it was some remote Scottish border castle. However it was later revealed, at closer quarters to be a Victorian hunting lodge, now used as a Youth Hostel, and we were then more attracted by Westerdale's single sloping street, with cottages and farmhouses looking out across to a small church... also mostly Victorian. Do not miss a glance from the road, at the Bulmer Monument, in the garden of Arkangel Cotage (see Route Directions). This commemorates Thomas Bulmer, a sailor who retired to here in 1727, with amusing verse describing his adventures. PLEASE DO NOT TRESPASS.

Westerdale is one of our favourite moorland villages, but while here, beware the shattering howl of R.A.F. jet aircraft, whose pilots seem intent in singling out this entrancing place for low level flying practice. We experienced this on three separate visits, and felt that Westerdale was receiving an unfair amount of attention.

Ralph Cross

Here on high Westerdale Moor (highest point 1409′), meet roads from Westerdale, Castleton, Rosedale and Hutton-le-Hole. It is a splendidly elemental place, especially at times when few fellow motorists are abroad... we once waited here on April 5th for snow ploughs to clear the road through to Rosedale (blocked since April 2nd), and had the bright sunlit moors almost to ourselves.

Ralph Cross is an 18th century replacement of a medieval cross, a dramatic reminder of difficult journeys across the moor in times past. Fat Betty, a short distance beyond, on the road to Rosedale, is a dumpy little medieval cross, coloured white and most aptly named.

Rosedale Abbey

Small village situated in beautiful Rosedale, beneath high Rosedale Chimney Bank (see page 11). It is grouped around a pleasant little triangular green, which is itself overlooked by an agreeable hotel, the Milburn Arms, with a small Victorian church beyond. This was built in 1839 by Lewis Vulliamy, the architect of magnificent Westonbirt in the far off Cotswolds, and contains an interesting 17th century carved lectern, believed to be of Dutch origin. Only a small fragment of the 12th century Cistercian nunnery remains (near the church).

John Hillaby author of those splendid classics 'Journey to the Jade Sea' and 'Journey through Britain' has a house in Rosedale (at the time of writing), and we can think of no better recommendation for Rosedale than this.

1. Westerdale Church

2. Ralph Cross

3. Rapid thaw beyond Ralph Cross

4. The Green, Rosedale Abbey

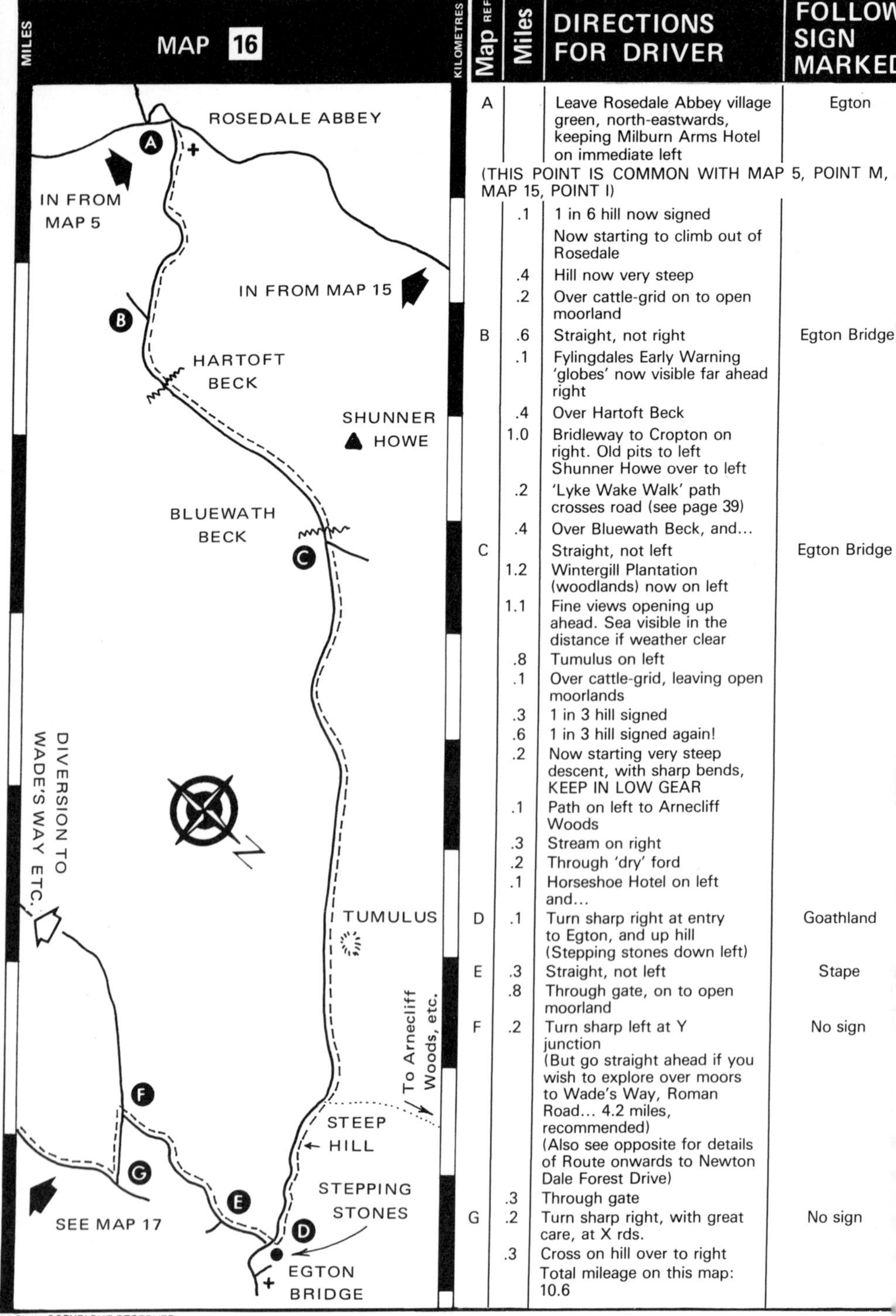

Map REF	Miles	DIRECTIONS FOR DRIVER	FOLLOW SIGN MARKED
A		Leave Rosedale Abbey village green, north-eastwards, keeping Milburn Arms Hotel on immediate left	Egton
(THIS POINT IS COMMON WITH MAP 5, POINT M, a MAP 15, POINT I)			
	.1	1 in 6 hill now signed	
		Now starting to climb out of Rosedale	
	.4	Hill now very steep	
	.2	Over cattle-grid on to open moorland	
B	.6	Straight, not right	Egton Bridge
	.1	Fylingdales Early Warning 'globes' now visible far ahead right	
	.4	Over Hartoft Beck	
	1.0	Bridleway to Cropton on right. Old pits to left Shunner Howe over to left	
	.2	'Lyke Wake Walk' path crosses road (see page 39)	
	.4	Over Bluewath Beck, and...	
C		Straight, not left	Egton Bridge
	1.2	Wintergill Plantation (woodlands) now on left	
	1.1	Fine views opening up ahead. Sea visible in the distance if weather clear	
	.8	Tumulus on left	
	.1	Over cattle-grid, leaving open moorlands	
	.3	1 in 3 hill signed	
	.6	1 in 3 hill signed again!	
	.2	Now starting very steep descent, with sharp bends, KEEP IN LOW GEAR	
	.1	Path on left to Arnecliff Woods	
	.3	Stream on right	
	.2	Through 'dry' ford	
	.1	Horseshoe Hotel on left and...	
D	.1	Turn sharp right at entry to Egton, and up hill (Stepping stones down left)	Goathland
E	.3	Straight, not left	Stape
	.8	Through gate, on to open moorland	
F	.2	Turn sharp left at Y junction (But go straight ahead if you wish to explore over moors to Wade's Way, Roman Road... 4.2 miles, recommended) (Also see opposite for details of Route onwards to Newton Dale Forest Drive)	No sign
	.3	Through gate	
G	.2	Turn sharp right, with great care, at X rds.	No sign
	.3	Cross on hill over to right	
		Total mileage on this map: 10.6	

PLACES OF INTEREST ON THE ROUTE

Fylingdales Early Warning Station

The 'radomes' of Fylingdales may be seen from several points on our route (see Route Directions). With the sun shining on their perfectly symmetrical, white surfaces, they lend excitement to the distant horizon. It is then possible to forget their sinister implications for a while, and think instead of 'stately pleasure domes'... some latter day Yorkshire Xanadu.

Shooting on the Moors

Beyond Point C there is a series of very smart circular gun butts in stone, looking rather like prehistoric hut circles that have been neatly restored by the Department of the Environment (e.g. Chysauster in Cornwall). The care with which these butts are built and maintained is evidence of the money spent to ensure that these moorlands provide good shooting during the relevant season. Whatever your views on this annual ritual of death, try to ensure that you give no offence to bird or man, as most of the North York Moors are privately owned, and could in theory still be barred at any time to all who wish to cross them.

Arnecliffe Woods and Beggar's Bridge

It is possible to walk through these woods from the road, first keeping above the Esk, and then dropping down to Beggar's Bridge, a pleasant 16th century structure near Glaisdale... about a mile in all.

Egton Bridge

Our route misses most of this small village, but there are stepping stones across the River Esk just beyond the attractive Horseshoe Hotel.

Wade's Causeway — Roman Road

A diversion of over four miles is required to visit Wade's Causeway by car, but this is strongly recommended. Our road across Wheeldale Moor is remote and unspoilt, and drops down to cross the Wheeldale Beck at a most attractive ford. There is three quarters of a mile of Roman Road in the care of the Department of the Environment, and it is most interesting. The rough nature of the road is due to the washing away of the top surfacing, thus revealing the larger foundation material. Do not overlook the drainage culverts, still complete with their capstones.

Beyond Wade's Causeway

There is a forest trackway beyond Wade's Way, and it is possible to walk south towards Snape, past Mauley Cross (a medieval wayside cross), and then due south to Pickering, linking with Map 4. This takes one through pleasant forest country bordered on the east by Newton Dale, up which runs the North York Moors Railway (See Page 35). See the Key Map, if you plan to walk along here, and if possible obtain a copy of the Ordnance Survey's North York Moors Tourist Map.

1. Our Road beyond Rosedale Abbey

2. Ford at Wheeldale Gill

3. Road to Wade's Causeway

4. Wade's Causeway Roman Road

MAP 17

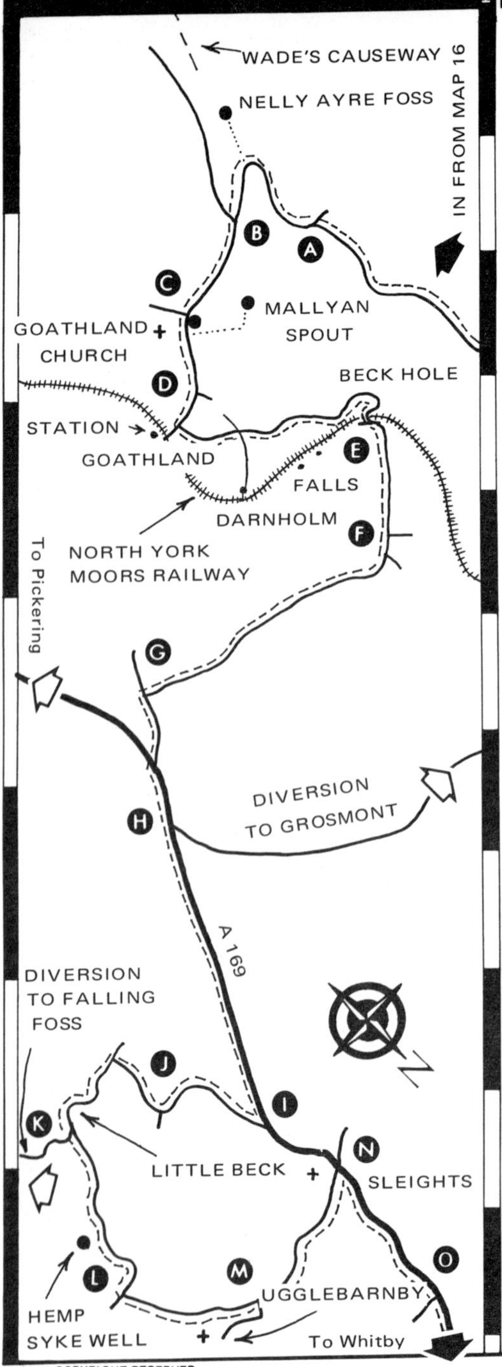

MILES

KILOMETRES

WADE'S CAUSEWAY
NELLY AYRE FOSS
IN FROM MAP 16
MALLYAN SPOUT
GOATHLAND CHURCH
BECK HOLE
STATION
GOATHLAND
FALLS
DARNHOLM
NORTH YORK MOORS RAILWAY
To Pickering
DIVERSION TO GROSMONT
A 169
DIVERSION TO FALLING FOSS
LITTLE BECK
SLEIGHTS
HEMP SYKE WELL
UGGLEBARNBY
To Whitby

Map ref	Miles	DIRECTIONS FOR DRIVER	FOLLOW SIGN MARKED
A	1.7	Bear left, by farm	No sign
	.3	Down steep narrow hill	
	.3	Path on right, to Nelly Ayre Force	
B	.3	Straight, not right (But turn right to visit Wade's Causeway)	Goathland
C	.5	Bear left by Goathland church, and hotel	No sign
		Path to Mallyan Spout to right hand of hotel	
D	.5	Bear right	Whitby
	.1	Turn left	Darnholm
	.4	Over diagonal X rds. (But turn right if you wish to visit Darnholm)	Beck Hole
	.4	Beck Hole entry signed	
	.2	Down steep hill	
	.2	Up 1 in 4 hill	
E	.1	Bear left beyond bridge	No sign
F	.8	Straight, not left, by phone box	No sign
	.1	Straight, not left	No sign
G	1.5	Bear left	Sleights
	.5	Turn left, on to A169	Sleights
H	.2	Straight, not left (But turn left to visit Grosmont Railway Station)	Whitby
	1.4	Car park on right	
I	.3	Turn sharp right with care, off A169 (But keep on A169, and link back to route at Point N, in Sleights, if you wish to avoid narrow circuitous route)	Little Beck
	.4	1 in 3 hill signed	
J	.3	Straight, not left	Little Beck
	.3	Little Beck entry signed	
	.1	Turn left at T junction	Little Beck
	.3	Down steep hill	
	.2	Turn left by chapel and...	
	.1	Over 'dry' ford	
K	.2	Straight, not right (But fork right to visit Falling Foss... 1.8)	Sneaton
	.5	Hemp Syke Well on right	
	.3	Bear right	No sign
L	.2	Turn left at T junction	Sleights
	.4	Ugglebarnby signed	
M	.4	Straight, not right	Sleights
	.7	Sleights entry signed	
N	.1	Turn right, beyond church, on to A169	Whitby
	.4	Whalebone arch on left	
O	.5	Straight, not right beyond bridge	Whitby
		NOT SHOWN ON MAP	
P	1.1	Turn right, on to A171	Whitby
Q	1.1	Over roundabout	Whitby
	.8	Straight, not left	Town Cent
	.2	Bear left	Piers, Bridg
	.2	Bear left, and...	
R		Turn right, over bridge	Scarboroug
	.2	Bear right	Scarboroug
S	.3	Turn left, at T junction	'To the Abb
	.4	Bear left at T junction	'Abbey'
T	.4	Arrive at Whitby Abbey	
(LINK HERE WITH MAP 1, POINT A)			
		Total mileage on this map: 19.8	

PLACES OF INTEREST ON THE ROUTE

Nelly Ayre Force

(See Route Directions for starting point.)

Take track immediately to left of house and follow beyond, keeping wall on right until it drops into valley... Nelly Ayre Force (waterfall) is just beyond.

Wade's Causeway — Roman Road

The northern end of the preserved section of Wade's Causeway (see page 33) is reached on foot from the end of our diversion at Point B... about a mile's walk, via Wheeldale Lodge Youth Hostel.

Goathland

Well known village scattered over widespread common land, close cropped by sheep, with a pleasant hotel looking across to the low towered late Victorian church. There is a path beside the hotel leading down to Mallyan Spout, a beautiful waterfall set in a deep valley, with trees and rocks in profusion. There is a station on the North Yorkshire Moors Railway at Goathland.

Darnholm

Turn right at diagonal cross roads beyond Goathland to visit the minute hamlet of Darnholm, with its shallow ford over the Eller Beck... a popular picnic place. (NO THROUGH ROAD.)

Beck Hole

Delightful hamlet in a deep valley. Walk up the valley from here to Water Ark Foss and Walker Mill Foss (waterfalls). Also beyond to Darnholm.

Grosmont Station and The North York Moors Railway

This railway runs between Grosmont and Pickering through 18 miles of moorland, farmland and forest. A daily service is operated from April 1 until the end of October using both steam and diesel motive power. Full details from Pickering Station.

Little Beck

Agreeable hamlet in a deep valley. It is possible to walk up the valley to Falling Foss from here.

Falling Foss

Set deeply in the woods, this attractive waterfall cascades almost vertically down a rock face into a tree shaded pool. There is a Forest Trail (3 miles or 1 mile).

Hemp Syke Well

Do not miss this little 'spring' at the roadside, complete with lion's head and typically devout Victorian verses. We wish we had room to quote...

Ugglebarnby

The church here was provided by Mr. J. Alan of Hempsyke in 1872, and is an example of Victorian church furnishing at its best.

Sleights

Has an unexceptional church and a whalebone archway beside the main road.

1. Mallyan Spout Hotel

2. Below Mallyan Spout

3. At Grosmont Station

4. Falling Foss Waterfall

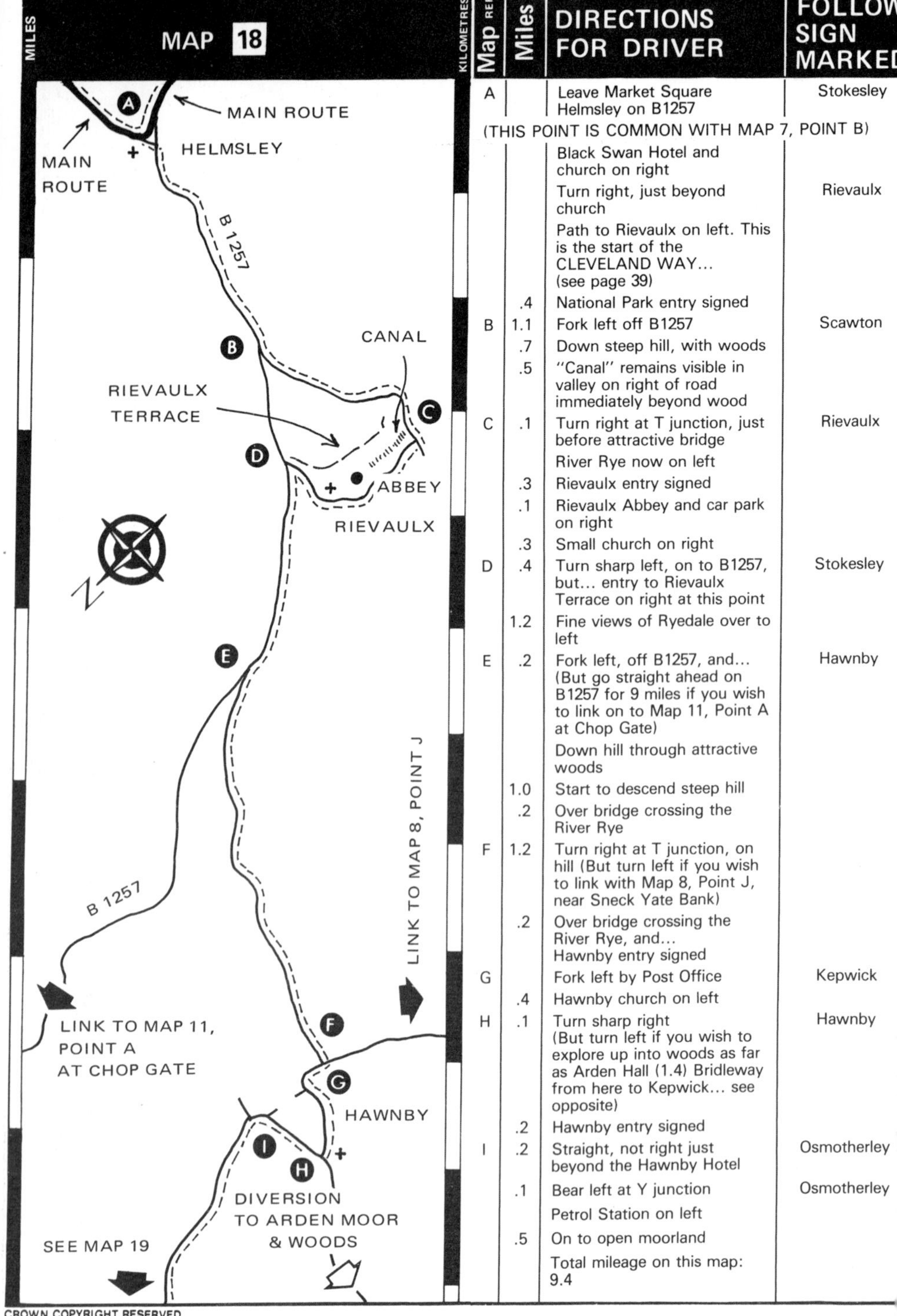

Map REF	Miles	DIRECTIONS FOR DRIVER	FOLLOW SIGN MARKED
A		Leave Market Square Helmsley on B1257	Stokesley
(THIS POINT IS COMMON WITH MAP 7, POINT B)			
		Black Swan Hotel and church on right	
		Turn right, just beyond church	Rievaulx
		Path to Rievaulx on left. This is the start of the CLEVELAND WAY... (see page 39)	
	.4	National Park entry signed	
B	1.1	Fork left off B1257	Scawton
	.7	Down steep hill, with woods	
	.5	"Canal" remains visible in valley on right of road immediately beyond wood	
C	.1	Turn right at T junction, just before attractive bridge	Rievaulx
		River Rye now on left	
	.3	Rievaulx entry signed	
	.1	Rievaulx Abbey and car park on right	
	.3	Small church on right	
D	.4	Turn sharp left, on to B1257, but... entry to Rievaulx Terrace on right at this point	Stokesley
	1.2	Fine views of Ryedale over to left	
E	.2	Fork left, off B1257, and... (But go straight ahead on B1257 for 9 miles if you wish to link on to Map 11, Point A at Chop Gate)	Hawnby
		Down hill through attractive woods	
	1.0	Start to descend steep hill	
	.2	Over bridge crossing the River Rye	
F	1.2	Turn right at T junction, on hill (But turn left if you wish to link with Map 8, Point J, near Sneck Yate Bank)	
	.2	Over bridge crossing the River Rye, and... Hawnby entry signed	
G		Fork left by Post Office	Kepwick
	.4	Hawnby church on left	
H	.1	Turn sharp right (But turn left if you wish to explore up into woods as far as Arden Hall (1.4) Bridleway from here to Kepwick... see opposite)	Hawnby
	.2	Hawnby entry signed	
I	.2	Straight, not right just beyond the Hawnby Hotel	Osmotherley
	.1	Bear left at Y junction	Osmotherley
		Petrol Station on left	
	.5	On to open moorland	
		Total mileage on this map: 9.4	

PLACES OF INTEREST ON THE ROUTE

Rievaulx

THE CANAL Earthworks of a canal built to bring building materials to Rievaulx Abbey, are clearly visible below the woods to our right as we enter the valley.

THE BRIDGE Graceful three arched bridge, built in the late 18th century.

THE ABBEY Rievaulx (Rye Vale) Abbey was colonised from the Cistercian Abbey of Clairvaulx in 1131, and was completed in just over a century. It had sadly declined by the time of the Dissolution, but enough remains of both church and monastic quarters to make this England's most impressive Cistercian Abbey, apart from Fountains. Like so many Cistercian foundations, it has a superb setting, and to appreciate this, it should certainly be viewed from the 'Terrace' above (see below), after it has been inspected at closer quarters.

THE VILLAGE The parish church was once the Abbey gatehouse chapel, but it was over restored in 1906.

RIEVAULX TERRACE A half mile of mown lawn, once part of Duncombe Park (see p. 15), with a classic temple at each end. This stretches along a hill-side, and although there are trees on both sides, those on the valley side are intersected by carefully contrived avenues, down which are obtained splendid views of the abbey, the Rye valley, and the rolling Yorkshire countryside beyond. This wonderful piece of landscape architecture was completed in 1758, and has since been the subject of a painting by Turner, and rapturous comments from William Cowper and Dorothy Wordsworth.

The Ionic Temple, at one end, has an interesting exhibition on English Landscape Design in the 18th century, in its basement.

Link to Sneck Yate Bank

Turn left at Point F, if you wish to link on to Map 8, Point J near the top of Sneck Yate Bank, by an attractive road up a wooded valley... about three miles.

Hawnby

Agreeable little stone village set in the beautifully wooded Rye valley... complete with cheerfully run Post Office stores and a comfortable looking hotel. The church is some distance from the village, delightfully situated in a churchyard with daffodils, with the River Rye just beyond. It is a small, mainly Norman building, with little bellcote and over restored Norman south doorway. There are two interesting 17th century wall monuments (Ralph Tankard and Ann Tankard), some imaginative stained glass, and a Norman (?) cross, which we found leaning up against the font.

Arden Hall

A gorgeous Queen Anne house situated at the very end of the public road in a beautifully wooded valley. It is not open to the public, but glimpses of its south front are visible from the road. There is a

Continued on Page 39

1. Rievaulx Abbey

2. Temple on Rievaulx Terrace

3. Rievaulx Abbey from the Terrace

4. Hawnby

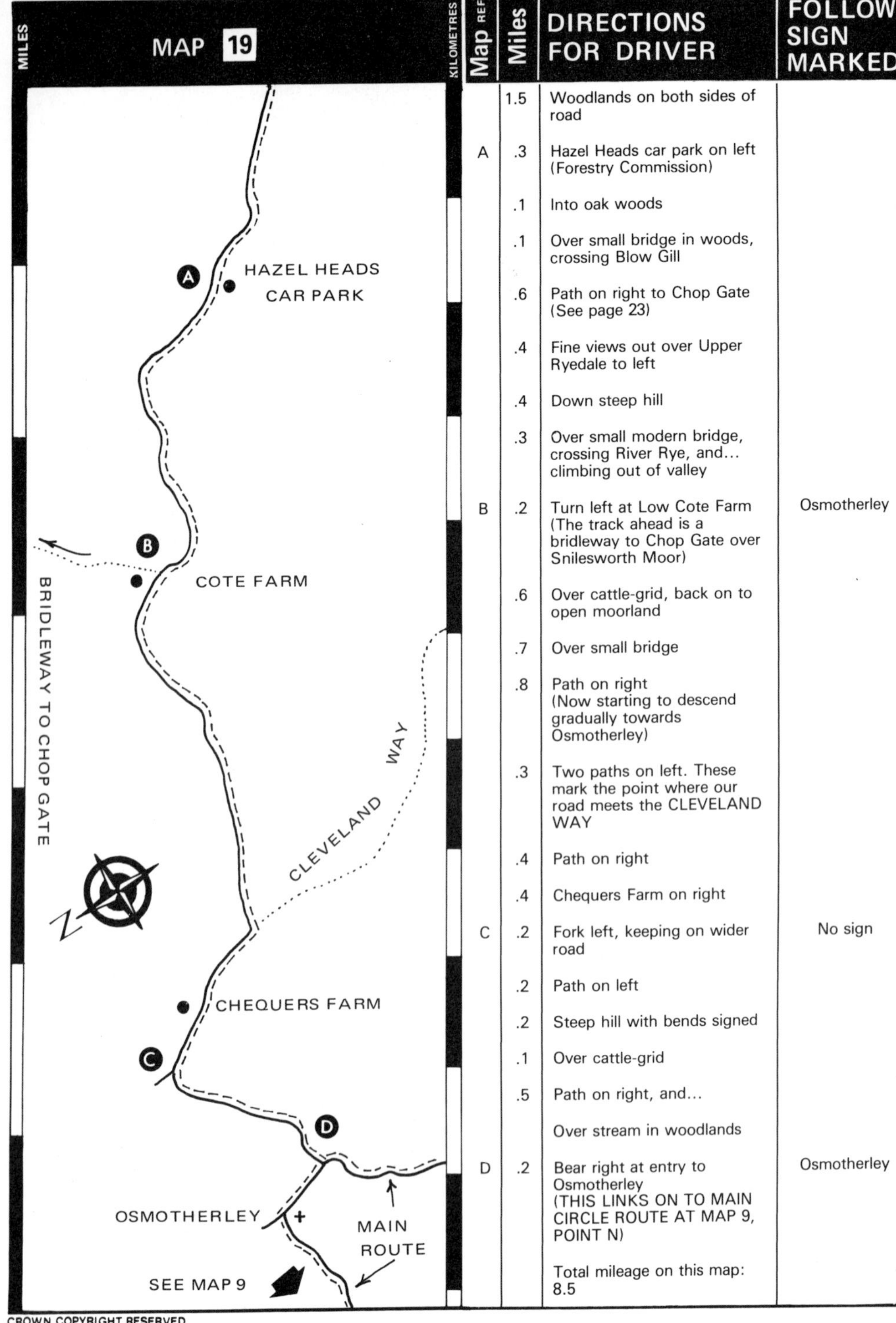

Map REF	Miles	DIRECTIONS FOR DRIVER	FOLLOW SIGN MARKED
	1.5	Woodlands on both sides of road	
A	.3	Hazel Heads car park on left (Forestry Commission)	
	.1	Into oak woods	
	.1	Over small bridge in woods, crossing Blow Gill	
	.6	Path on right to Chop Gate (See page 23)	
	.4	Fine views out over Upper Ryedale to left	
	.4	Down steep hill	
	.3	Over small modern bridge, crossing River Rye, and... climbing out of valley	
B	.2	Turn left at Low Cote Farm (The track ahead is a bridleway to Chop Gate over Snilesworth Moor)	Osmotherley
	.6	Over cattle-grid, back on to open moorland	
	.7	Over small bridge	
	.8	Path on right (Now starting to descend gradually towards Osmotherley)	
	.3	Two paths on left. These mark the point where our road meets the CLEVELAND WAY	
	.4	Path on right	
	.4	Chequers Farm on right	
C	.2	Fork left, keeping on wider road	No sign
	.2	Path on left	
	.2	Steep hill with bends signed	
	.1	Over cattle-grid	
	.5	Path on right, and...	
		Over stream in woodlands	
D	.2	Bear right at entry to Osmotherley (THIS LINKS ON TO MAIN CIRCLE ROUTE AT MAP 9, POINT N)	Osmotherley
		Total mileage on this map: 8.5	

PLACES OF INTEREST ON THE ROUTE

Arden Hall *continued*
bridle road from here, up through the woods, and over the moors, to Kepwick...about three miles (see page 19).

Upper Ryedale — and over to Osmotherley
In the course of nine miles, our road from Hawnby to Osmotherley, climbs up out of Ryedale, through Hazel Heads Wood, and finally out over the top of Osmotherley Moor... nearly 950′ above sea level at one point. It passes a few farms and cottages, but goes through no village, or feature of outstanding interest. However it is a fine moorland run, and we hope that lack of features will not deter you from making use of Map 19.

Osmotherley (see also page 20)
Once a market town, Osmotherley is now a large village, and lies quietly beneath the moors. It is centred upon a triangular green, with a few shops looking across to a market cross and a stone table, once used as a pulpit by John Wesley. The church, approached up a narrow passage beside the Queen Catherine, has a Norman south doorway, with an Anglo-Danish 'hog-back' tombstone and fragments of a cross shaft in the porch. The interior of the church has been over-restored.

GENERAL NOTES

The Cleveland Way
Officially opened in 1969, this is now one of England's finest Long Distance Footpaths. It stretches from Helmsley, around the western edges of the Yorkshire Moors to Saltburn, and then down the coast to Scarborough... a total distance of nearly 100 miles. It is marked, where it leaves or joins a road with the signs MOORS PATH or COAST PATH and away from the roads it is marked with the distinctive Acorn symbol (see above). For details we would recommend *The Cleveland Way* published by H.M.S.O., especially as it incorporates 2½″ maps of the whole route.

The Lyke Wake Walk
This is a forty mile 'walk' across the moors from Scarth Wood (north of Osmotherley) to Ravenscar on the coast (or vice-versa). It was instituted by Mr. Bill Cowley in 1965, and is now a firmly established feature, although it is still not a right of way. For details of the walk and the Lyke Wake Club, we can do no better than recommend Mr. Cowley's book on the subject *Lyke Wake Walk*, published by the Dalesman Publishing Company.

Walking on The North York Moors
The area covered by this guide contains some of the finest walking country in Britain, and there is scope for even the most inexperienced walkers, in the dales. However before setting out to cross the high moorlands, ensure that you have proper clothing, equipment and advice. If in doubt read the leaflet available from the National Park Centres on *Walking on the North York Moors*. Always carry the Ordnance Survey's One Inch Tourist Edition Map of the North York Moors.

1. Hazel Heads Car Park

2. Farm in Upper Ryedale

3. Upper Ryedale

4. Moorland Road to Osmotherley

INDEX